LOVE AND MAYHEM

ONE BIG FAMILY'S UPLIFTING STORY OF FOSTERING AND ADOPTION

JOHN DEGARMO

Jessica Kingsley *Publishers*
London and Philadelphia

First published in 2015
by Jessica Kingsley Publishers
73 Collier Street
London N1 9BE, UK
and
400 Market Street, Suite 400
Philadelphia, PA 19106, USA

www.jkp.com

Library of Congress Cataloging in Publication Data
DeGarmo, John, 1969-
Love and mayhem : one big family's uplifting story of
fostering and adoption / John DeGarmo.
pages cm
ISBN 978-1-84905-775-2 (alk. paper)
1. Foster parents. 2. Foster children. 3. Parenting. I. Title.
HQ759.7.D445 2014   306.874--dc23   2014010418

British Library Cataloguing in Publication Data
A CIP catalogue record for this book is available from the British Library

ISBN 978 1 84905 775 2
eISBN 978 1 78450 012 2

Printed and bound in Great Britain

For Jessica, who we continue to search for, and for David,
who has come so very far from such horrors.

Truly I tell you, whatever you did for one of the least of these brothers and sisters of mine, you did for me.

(Matthew 25:40)

CONTENTS

ACKNOWLEDGMENTS

Thank you to my friend Zeljko Gataric-Imhoff, whose help in the first memoir was instrumental. Thank you also to my wife Kelly, whose love of children is inspiring. Finally, thank you to my editor Stephen Jones, who continues to support my writing.

PREFACE

This book follows on from my first memoir, *Fostering Love: One Foster Parent's Journey*, which described my first nine years as a foster parent, and leads up to the first chapter of this book. The book you have in your hands describes the continuing journey and adventure of being a foster parent, and how I have grown as a person from it.

Foster parenting a large family has its fair share of joys and challenges, and can be emotionally draining. Indeed, at times, it has been exhausting and fulfilling; full of sadness while also full of elation. Foster and adoptive parents have to draw deep from a well, a well that provides them strength and grace. If not, they can quickly wear out, or burn out. Indeed, as I travel across the United States, speaking to my fellow foster and adoptive parents, I listen to many who share with me that they had become burned out, due to the high levels of stress and exhaustion they faced while taking care of children in need.

For me, this source of strength has been my faith. I have found that my faith has given me the strength I have needed when I felt I could no longer continue as a foster parent. Along with this, I have also found that my faith had surrounded me with people who felt led to help our children in foster care through various means. For others, their source of strength may be a foster parent association or close friends, finding solace in art or nature, exercising, or writing in a journal. Whatever it might be, foster and adoptive parents share the one same goal, to help a child who is suffering, to provide a home for a child who is in want, and to bring love to a child who may need it the most.

On any given day, there are over 500,000 children placed in foster care in the United States alone. Each of these children has suffered immeasurable hurt, unimaginable pain, and unspeakable horrors from those who were supposed to love them the most. The life of a child in foster care has been one of great pain and tremendous suffering. For many of these children, a stable home and a loving family is all they crave, yet never truly find. More often than not, these children in care never truly recover from the emotional, physical, and psychological wounds that they suffer from.

In writing this book about our lives, I have tried to describe some of the stories that the children in care have gone through while living in my home, as well as how their stories and their lives have affected my own family. Each of these children who has come into my home has allowed my own family to grow in love, as we dedicated our lives to care for them. For that, I am grateful; for that I am blessed. May you also find a way to help children in need, and may you find the joy that only children can bring.

For the children,
John DeGarmo

Chapter 1

I was exhausted. It had only been five days since the three foster children had come to live with us, yet I was tired, so very tired. It felt like I had been sleep walking through the past few days. Frankly, it felt like I was on exhaust fumes, as there simply was not much energy left in my tank. I think I realized this while I was at church earlier that morning when Mary Lou told me that I looked tired. I was dog tired, and cat tired, as well. That is, if cats ever became tired. If they did, I was tired for all nine of their lives.

Kelly, my Australian-born wife of 16 years, and I had been foster parents for nine years. During that time, we had been foster parents to 21 children, including Micah, Joshua, and Linda, who had arrived in our home only recently. With our own four children, our house was indeed full. A friend of mine at church, Robby, often joked with me that it was dangerous to have the number of children in a house outnumber the number of adults. I had long since thrown that advice to the wind, as there were seven children and two adults in our home. We had equaled the Brady Bunch in terms of size, to be precise, if you included Alice the maid. Sadly, we had no maid, and our house showed it. We sure could use an Alice to help with the cleaning, the cooking, the dishes, the laundry, and just another adult voice of sanity in the midst of children-filled chaos.

It was four in the morning, and it was the third time I had been up with Linda. It was my night to be on duty, as Kelly was up last night with her. I tried to tiptoe quietly out of the bedroom, so as not to disturb my slumbering wife, though I knew that she was probably awake, as well, suffering from another of her migraines. The baby's crib lay near our own bed, while her 18-month-old brother Joshua's crib was in the parlor, and three-year-old Micah was asleep downstairs in the spare bedroom. Micah had just fallen asleep a few hours earlier, as he once again cried himself to sleep from the heartbreak of being separated from his mother. The poor child; my own heart ached for him, as I felt such sorrow for his plight.

Through our years as foster parents, Kelly and I had found that the first few nights and weeks were often the most difficult with children in foster care. After all, these children in need are placed into care against their will. They are taken from their mothers, their fathers, their families, their homes, their friends and neighbors, and even their schools; taken away from all they know and that is familiar to them. Instead, they are placed into a home that is strange to them, with foster parents that are strangers to them, and told that this will be their new home with their new family. Micah, like so many before him, spent his first nights in our home crying uncontrollably when he went to bed, missing his mother so terribly. The poor boy was not only heartbroken for his mother; he was frightened, confused, and scared. He was living with strangers, in a strange home, and did not know why. Was it his fault? Did his mother not love him anymore? Where was she? Would he ever see her again? These thoughts surely filled his young head at night, wracking his small body with such emotional turmoil that I could only imagine.

I, on the other hand, felt anger towards his mother. How could parents be so cruel towards their own children? In Linda's, Micah's, and Joshua's case, their mother had not only neglected the children, she had beaten her own son, Joshua, with an electrical cord on several occasions. His father, like the father of the other two children, was nowhere to be found.

As a result of all of this, Joshua was the angriest human being I had ever come across. Such rage, such anger I had never experienced, and it was truly frightening. Perhaps the most disturbing aspect of his rage was the fact that he was so young, so very young. I shuddered when thinking of his future, a future that whispered of hostility and even of danger. I felt such compassion towards these children, towards all foster children.

Not only was the four-month-old baby girl crying for her bottle, her wheezing broke the quiet of the night. Linda suffered terribly from Respiratory Syncytial Virus, or RSV, a sickness that I was not familiar with before she and her two brothers had come to live with us just a few short days ago. I learned quickly, though, that RSV was a virus that caused an infection in the lungs and breathing passages, and that it could be serious for young children. Linda already suffered from poor nutrition and had not developed a strong immune system. As a result, the baby needed to be treated every two hours or so. Kelly or I were usually up at ten, midnight, two, and four a.m., and gave her another treatment before we headed off to work each morning. It was indeed exhausting.

It was difficult to listen to Linda's crying, as it was mixed with her wheezing. She had such a grueling time breathing, and there was very little we could do for her, outside of her treatment. Closing the bedroom door, I turned the kitchen light on, and prepared her a bottle through half-closed eyelids from lack of sleep.

"Shhh," I whispered, as I crept back into the bedroom with her bottle. Bending down to pick her up, I checked to see if her diaper needed changing. "Thank goodness," I said to myself silently, as a sigh of relief escaped from my lips. No diaper change; a tiny victory for me.

Closing the bedroom door again, I carried Linda to the lounge room where her breathing machine was kept. Pouring the medicine into the top container of the nebulized bronchodilator, or ventilator machine, I turned it on, and placed the tubing over her face. The tiny baby breathed in the vapors from the mist while curled in my lap. The vapors helped to open up the air passages in her lungs, helping her to breathe easier, while an anti-viral agent helped to combat the virus infecting her small body. As the house was cold from the November winter, I covered us both with one of the homemade quilts Kelly made for our older children years ago.

"Lord, please heal this tiny child of Yours," I prayed silently to myself, with tears welling in my eyes. "She has already had so much going against her. Please hold her in Your arms of grace and mercy. Amen."

Thirty minutes later, the ventilator indicated that the chamber that the medicine had been in was empty, and Linda began to cry out again, minus the wheezing for the moment. It was bottle time, as I once again had to keep Mr. Sandman and his call to sleep at bay.

When I lay back down again, I was disappointed to see that the Mickey Mouse alarm clock next to my bed read 5:20. Forty minutes until the alarm rang. Once again, a good night's sleep was to elude me. Maybe this morning was the day I should start drinking coffee, as I sure did need a boost of energy to get me through the approaching day.

* * *

"G'day, Boomie." Kelly greeted me with her nickname for me, and in a typical Australian hello, as I walked into the house after the work day was over. My job as the local high school's, librarian or media specialist as the new 21st-century education lingo called it, allowed me to be home around 4:30 each afternoon. Indeed, Kelly's own job also saw her home most afternoons, as well. She had been blessed with a very successful career as a massage therapist. Along with her career as a doctor of nutrition, Kelly was always in demand from her clients who looked to her for not only pain relief from her massages, but also for her warmth, love, and Aussie charm.

"Hey, Sweetheart," I said, giving her a kiss on the cheek, as she took Linda from my arms.

"Hi Micah! Hi Joshua!" My daughter Jace met both with a large grin, sweeping both of them up in her arms, giving both of them a kiss. As Micah had some developmental delay issues, common in so many foster children, his speech was limited to really only one or two words at a time. As a result, he simply looked up at Jace with his infectious smile. Joshua laughed aloud, and seemed to really enjoy Jace's attention. Our middle daughter, aged 11, Jace was an integral part of our foster family, as were her older sister Kolby, aged 12, and their younger brother Brody, aged 10—helping to keep the house clean, feed babies, change diapers, play with foster children, and, most importantly, love children who were in such need. Kelly and I would never be able to foster if our own children were not willing to help out by taking these children into their own lives, year after year, child after child.

"Hi Daddy."

"Hey, birthday girl. Happy birthday! How is my four-year-old doing?" I asked, as I rushed over to the kitchen table, giving four-year-old Grace a hug and kiss. Grace came to live with us as a foster child when she was five days old. After 20 months in our home, during which many lengthy and bruising court battles were waged, many phone calls were made to lawyers and even a judge, and a few very close calls which would have seen the little one sent to another home, as well as to a biological grandmother unfit to care for her, Grace was adopted into our home as our fourth child. With her formally becoming a member of the DeGarmo family, she had brought much fun, love, and plenty of drama during her four short years of life with us.

"I'm good, Daddy. Kolby and Brody are helping me get ready for my party," she said, her dark skin easily masking the birthday chocolate smeared across her face. Giving Kolby and Brody a kiss hello, I joined Kelly in the kitchen as she readied the meal, along with the ice-cream cake.

"Boomie, we need to talk about Joshua soon. He really should see a doctor of some sort for his anger. Last night was just as bad as all the rest." It had been a month since Linda, Joshua, and Micah had come to live with us, and Kelly and I had had very little time to ourselves.

"I agree; I've never seen anything like this, before, Kelly. And it doesn't seem to be stopping any, either." I looked over at Joshua. He was smiling at the moment, showing no indication of the angry little boy that usually resided in our home. Young Joshua had the sad tendency to hit anything that would walk by him, including my own children. As he was indeed so very young, it was particularly sad as he had learned to do this from someone else, probably watching someone in his home hit others on a daily basis. Perhaps it was the result of his own mother beating him with the electrical cord. How could someone so young suffer so terribly? How could someone so young also learn such horrific habits? These questions disturbed me greatly, as they often weighed heavily in my head, and in my heart.

Each evening, when placed into his crib, Joshua would shake his crib, screaming with a rage that no child should ever have in his body. So strong was his eruption of anger, his crib would move across the length of the room from his shaking. He had been doing this each evening until he would collapse from exhaustion into a slumber, despite all attempts from Kelly and me to pacify his fury. As we were powerless to help the young 18-month-old, these fits of anger would sometimes last up to two hours at a time. All we could do was hold on, hold on to our sanity and our patience, all the while praying for him. Our own four children had become rather weary of his fits, though they continued to minister to him and his siblings with love, compassion, and playfulness.

Joshua, the young dynamo, would greet each day with the same demonstration, announcing to all the world that he no longer wished to be kept in his crib. As our house was surrounded by forest, I greatly preferred being woken by the chorus of birds that enveloped our home, or even by the roosters in our backyard menagerie of animals. Joshua felt otherwise, apparently, and decided to announce his intentions in his own way. In the past, Grace was often the first up, waking at the first hint of sunshine peering through the trees. Joshua, though, would often begin his screaming fits around 4:30 a.m., usually as he grew hungry. As he had recently found a way to climb out of his crib, Kelly or I would have to scramble out of bed and prevent him from wreaking havoc in the house.

As often as not, I had found that God has a remarkable sense of humor, and enjoys shaking things up to remind us that He is in charge. This was quite evident the following day. The morning started out like all the rest, of late. We had become experts of sorts at getting four children ready for school each morning. As Micah was also in diapers, like his brother and sister, the addition of three children was more than challenging; it bordered on mayhem. The DeGarmo home had truly become a three-ring circus, with Kelly and I hapless ringleaders. As Micah had an intestinal problem with his bowels, he would need a bathing each morning, as he would soil himself beyond human description. Couple this with his developmental delays, and Micah was simply behind the average child his age. Adding to this pandemonium was Joshua's usual crabby demeanor each morning. Linda was a four-month-old baby, and needed the attention a four-month-old requires, a bottle, a fresh diaper, and an occasional bath. As Kelly and I were trying to get ready for work, ourselves, each morning, along with the other four children, the mornings were often straight from a comical episode of a dysfunctional family from the latest reality show that so many seemed to enjoy. In fact, Kelly and I had been told many a time that our lives would be the right fit for such a television program. The thought of this seemed amusing enough.

What made the day one for the memory books occurred after I left work. It had been one of those days, one of those rare days, at work that had left me done in, beat, and exhausted. Most days, I found my job to be a time that was relaxing and refreshing, as the hard work occurred at home each evening, with cooking, cleaning, dirty clothes, homework, and the general toil that can come with seven children and two adults in the home. On this day, though, my job left me drained. After a school-wide faculty meeting, I rushed out of the building and headed off to pick up the three younger children at day care. As the faculty meeting ran late, I was running late, as well. In fact, I was 20 minutes late picking up Brody and Kolby from piano lessons.

We arrived home much later than I wanted, and had only an hour and a half before we were to be back at church for the monthly family night supper. As Kelly was at work late this evening, I relished the opportunity to take seven children to church, as I knew that the dinner there would be better than anything I could ever whip up. I knew my limitations, and had grown to accept that cooking was not a talent that I would ever come to embrace, though I did make a mean bowl of Fruity Pebbles.

Kolby and Brody had already exited the car and had gone inside to begin homework. Grace closed the door behind her and headed down the driveway to feed the chickens, ducks, and turkeys; our small zoo of pets that we had gathered together in the hope that animal therapy would help the foster children who came through our home. As I closed my car door behind me, walking to the other side to let out Micah and Joshua before picking up the baby bags and Linda, I heard a sound that I immediately recognized as the knell from the dreaded Doomsday Bell, tolling for me. It was the click, the click of dread, the click of the car lock. The car had locked! With three foster children inside, the car had locked! The day had suddenly grown worse, much worse.

With a groan that made the ground tremble beneath me, I dropped the baby bag, standing frozen in place, appreciating the doom that I was placed in. As Kelly and I lived so far out in "the sticks," so to speak, we seldom brought the car keys into the house, instead leaving them in the car. This was the cause of my mighty groan, and of the colossal sigh that shook the remaining fall leaves from the winter branches. Normally, I would simply walk back into the house and retrieve the extra set of keys for the car. My earth-shattering groan and immense sigh was for the realization that these keys, keys that would unlock this calamity, were in Kelly's purse at this very moment. This was certainly not an event that I wanted to report to my children's caseworker, nor to the Department of Family and Children Services, or DFCS, our state of Georgia's child welfare agency. Foster parents were generally not encouraged to lock their foster children in cars. I was sure not to win any Foster Parent of the Year Award from child welfare agencies the nation over, as surely this action, the action of locking foster children in a car, was frowned upon.

Micah's innocent smile was spread across his face, while Joshua and Linda were looking at me from inside the car, all three locked into their car seats. Perhaps, I thought, Micah can deliver us from this misfortune. Placing my face against the car window, I called out to him.

"Micah, push the button. Push the button, son." Pointing towards the button that would unlock the car door, I urged Micah to push it. His right hand was easily within reach of it, and I felt that we would all be inside within a moment or two. "Just push the button, Micah."

"What are you doing, Daddy?" Grace asked, as she walked back up the driveway from feeding the animals.

"Oh, Daddy's just trying to get the children out of the car before dinner," I said, between gritted teeth. "Now, go in the house please, Sweetie, and ask Kolby to run a bath for you and the others, please."

Returning my attention back to the disaster in hand, I again pointed to the button, imploring Micah to unlock the car. For 20 long minutes, I begged, I persuaded, I demanded. "Micah, would you please push the button? The button right by your hand. Your hand, Micah, your hand. Yes, push *that* button." By this time, Linda began to cry, no doubt hungry, as it was well past five in the evening. As I feared, Joshua soon joined in, lending his cry to hers in a duet. I had to get them out of the car before Micah made it a trio. Pleading to him, I raised

my voice, slowly advising the three-year-old, "Push...the...
button...*please!*" This last word was drawn out, holding such
urgency that it caused Micah to break out in tears, as well. All
was indeed lost. As I began to appreciate the comedy of this
error, I broke out in sad laughter, my head leaning against the
window. It was time to call in the reserves.

Fifteen minutes later, the locksmith arrived to save the day.
By this point, all three children were not only crying, they were
in full screaming mode. Fortunately, the locksmith had them
out in a few minutes. When asked how much it cost to have
him drive out to my home and free the children from their
automobile-induced prison, the locksmith kindly told me
that it was on the house. "After all," the grey-haired kind older
gentleman said, "it's the least I can do. You all are taking care of
these children. Not many would do that." His deep smile and
kind gesture suddenly had me swallow down the tears I knew
could soon break forth. Such kindness and such generosity
were overwhelming. During the past eight years as a foster
parent, I had seen these acts many times beforehand. From
church members, from neighbors, and even from strangers,
these acts of kindness never ceased to surprise me.

In fact, it wasn't long after that two more acts of kindness
were showered upon Kelly and me. It was a few weeks before
Christmas when Kelly came home from work. Carrying
two bags in her hands, her face lit up like one of the shiniest
ornaments on our 12-foot Christmas tree that stood in the
lounge room. "What is it?" I enquired of her, as she seemed
about to bust.

"Mary Lou gave us these gifts for the three foster children,"
she beamed. "She let the foster parents in town go to the
church to pick up some toys for the foster children. I was
able to get some neat things for Linda, Joshua, and Micah."
For ten years or so, Mary Lou Jordan had worked tirelessly
from July to Christmas, finding resources to provide for needy
children in the county as they head back to school with school
supplies, as well as for Christmas time with clothes, shoes, and
a gift. It was an incredible effort, and one that our church had

supported in an all-out effort to ease the burdens of those in the area who were suffering from poverty. Mary Lou's heart for children was an inspiration to both Kelly and me.

Three nights later, I arrived home with the three little ones. Kelly had the other four in her car, and had run to pick up some groceries. We had enjoyed an evening out, watching Kolby play in her middle school's band concert. As we had nine in the house, we had become a two-car family, not being able to fit all in one car safely. Pulling up to the driveway, I was met by a great many bags and boxes sitting in front of the door. As it was late, and both Linda and Joshua were already asleep, I took the two children into the house, with Micah following close behind. Fifteen minutes later, when all were in bed, I brought the bags and boxes inside, curious as to not only the contents, but where they came from, as well. Bringing the last box into the house, Kelly and the kids also walked in, carrying in a load of groceries fit for the army of seven children that slept under our roof.

"What's that?" my bride asked, stopping to kiss me on the cheek.

"Well, it looks to be a lot of clothes," I remarked, with a puzzled grin on my face. "There's also a whole bunch of toys, too, but I have absolutely no idea where they came from. They were sitting in front of the door when I got home." Placing her load of groceries on the floor, Kelly knelt down beside me to look at this early Christmas present, while the other four children went upstairs with their loads. As we were investigating this Christmas mystery, the phone rang. Quickly answering it, Kelly's voice held such excitement in it, laughing and raising her voice in delight.

"That was our neighbor, Rebah," she said, placing the phone back in its receiver. "All those bags are from her, and..."

"What?" I interrupted. "That's incredible! What do you mean, they're all from her?" I was stunned. There must have been at least eight garbage-sized bags full of clothes and toys.

"I know," Kelly replied with a grin. "I can't believe it myself. Rebah told some people at her church last week that we had three foster children, and their story. She said that they were so touched by this that they wanted to help out in some way. Boomie, there's enough clothes and toys in here to last these children a long time. People are so generous," she said, with tears coming to her own eyes. Kelly had always been more emotional than me, crying at even the sappiest commercials on TV. I, on the other hand, was rather new to the whole crying at the drop of a hat thing. Time and time again, I have been amazed at how people have reached out to us and to our foster children, helping in ways that always seemed to be a blessing to our family at just the right time.

* * *

Christmas had come and gone, and we were soon into the second month of the new year of 2011. During this time, we had battled Joshua's anger, Linda's breathing problems, and Micah's intestinal bowel issues, and were the worse for wear. The daily routine of taking care of four other children as well was tiring enough. Kelly and I were as exhausted as we had ever been as foster parents. Add to this the letters that we had received from the three children's biological mother, letters that told us that we were poor foster parents, that we were not raising her children properly, and letters filled with instructions on how to better parent them. If we were not careful, Kelly and I were heading toward a state of near depression. Fortunately, the second snowfall of the year had brought just what we needed.

Though we did have a snowfall on Christmas night, snow in our part of middle Georgia was quite rare. As a child growing up in the tundra that is Michigan, I was quite used to snow, feet and feet of snow, and I was disappointed that my own children could not experience the joys that came along with it. Sledding, skating, snowman assembly, and even a good old fashioned snowball fight were part of my cherished memories as a child. Mid January brought a good four inches to our home one Saturday afternoon. Before Kelly and I could tell the four oldest children to be careful, they were out the door, bundled in a rag-tag collection of jackets, hats, shoes, and two pairs of pants. Kelly gathered together some warm weather clothing of Grace's and Brody's for both Micah and Joshua, with the clothes practically hanging off them, too big for their tiny frames. Soon afterwards, with Linda in Kelly's arms, I dashed out to join the six children. Momentarily, we were building our own snowmen, throwing a few snowballs, and sledding down our steep hill of a driveway on improvised sleds. An hour and a half later, we all re-entered the house, a mixture of laughing, shivering, and tired. All slept well that night from exhaustion, even Joshua.

* * *

"Kelly, Susan just called me; the children are going back to live with their mother tomorrow." After leaving the message on Kelly's answering machine, I sat back in my chair, disheartened from the conversation I had just had with the children's caseworker. She had called me at work, informing me that the three children were to move back home with their mother. It was a difficult conversation, one in which I no doubt came across as the bad guy, so to speak. Their mother had gotten a job at a local fast-food restaurant, and, in the eyes of DFCS, was now able to appropriately take care of her children.

I protested to her, "Susan, when I take foster children into my home, they become my children. I fight for them as if they were my own." I had told her just moments before on the phone, "I wonder if this young mother will be able to provide for them all that they need. How can someone who is so young, and by herself, make sure that Micah, who has severe learning disabilities, and Joshua, who has anger issues, get the resources they need to thrive? Kelly and I have struggled enough by ourselves to provide what these children require. How can she do this, by herself? Besides this, it was just a few months ago that she was beating them with an electrical cord. Are you telling me that because she has a job now, she no longer has these issues?" I was frustrated, and I was concerned. I just didn't want to see these children placed back in an environment where they would take steps backwards, where they would suffer. My phone call did nothing to change the situation, though I did feel better knowing that I at least tried. After all, every child needs someone to fight for them.

Yet, at the same time, I knew that I was being judgmental, that I was judging this lady, whom I had never met. It was terribly unfair of me, I recognized, and I was ashamed of it. I just had such a difficult time believing that this decision was the best one for these children. In fact, Kelly and I both believed that the children would eventually be returned back into foster care, as so many children often are. With this in mind, I made the request to Susan to have the opportunity to have them placed in our home again, if only for the sake of consistency for the children.

Two days later, I dropped the children off at their day care, along with their clothes and belongings. Susan was to pick them up later in the day and return them to their home in what is known in foster care as "reunification," or the reuniting of a foster child with a biological parent or family member. Like all the rest, this was a difficult time for our family, as we had become quite attached to them, despite the exhaustion we felt. In fact, this was a particularly difficult separation for Kelly.

Kelly had grown to love each child individually, though she had developed a special love for baby Linda. This tiny infant, so very precious and so very helpless, had wrapped herself around Kelly's heart. Perhaps it was Kelly's mothering instinct, perhaps it was the hours and hours of treatment each evening and morning, perhaps it was simply that Kelly, like many mothers, loved babies. Yet, when it was time for Kelly to give the baby one last kiss, she did so, with tears streaming down her face.

The next moment was more difficult, though, for my wife. After placing Joshua down from a farewell kiss and hug, she leaned over to scoop up Micah in her arms. What came from his lips next was nothing less than a miracle, leaving Kelly stunned.

"I love you, Mommy."

Four words; four simple words that Kelly had heard her own children say to her countless times throughout each day. Four words Kelly had heard many other foster children tell her, as well, throughout the past eight years. Yet, from Micah, these very words shook Kelly so emotionally that she could only hug the boy all the harder, drawing him into her chest tightly as she embraced him deeply. Micah, who had only been able to speak no more than two words at a time, spoke volumes to Kelly that moment. The little three-year-old boy, who had never spoken the words "love" or "Mommy" before, had reassured to Kelly that, despite the difficulties, being a foster parent to these children was not only worth it, but that she had made a positive impact in their lives.

Struggling to compose herself from the overwhelming surge of emotions that threatened to envelop her, Kelly managed to utter, "Oh, Micah, I love you, too." Wiping away the tears that cascaded from her own face like a brook, she took the young boy's face in her hands, giving him a kiss on each cheek, and hugging him even tighter to her own body. After one final moment, she helped me place all three children into their car seats. With Kolby, Jace, Brody, and Grace standing next to her, she waved along with them as I drove out of the driveway to the day care.

"Mommy, do you think we will ever see them again?" Brody asked.

"I hope so, Sweetheart, I hope so."

Chapter 2

If I was told when I was younger that I would one day become a foster parent to over two dozen children, I would have looked at the person with a great deal of skepticism along with some amusement. There are those who say that being a foster parent is the hardest thing you could ever do. Indeed, it is not only hard work, it is heart work. Foster parenting is a job that has changed my life in so many ways, as I have opened my house, my life, and my heart to children in need. Indeed, there are those times where I would often struggle with fostering, as well as struggle with my own self. Often times, I would be disappointed in my own foster parenting skills, as well as my habit of judging the birth parents. Yet, both Kelly and I felt called to take care of these children, so many children in need.

When I first met Kelly, she was simply Kelly from Australia, one of 165 other people from 25 different countries, traveling and performing in the international performing group Up With People. Up With People, a global organization that toured throughout the world over a course of a year, had the goal of bridging cultural barriers and global understanding through service and music. Throughout that year of 1990, we toured across the USA, Japan, Bermuda, and various European countries, all the while helping out with community service, working alongside people from all parts of the world, and performing in an uplifting and inspirational two-hour song and dance show, with songs from across the globe. During our year, Kelly and I, along with our fellow performers, performed in front of kings and queens, world dignitaries, movie stars, professional athletes, and entertainers from all parts of the globe. We visited the recently fallen Berlin Wall, each taking a hammer and chisel to it, and even performed on *Good Morning America* and many other television shows around the world. It was a sensational year, a year in which I gained a better appreciation of the world around me, the appreciation of cultural differences and traditions, all while forming close friendships with people from every corner of the globe. It was a year of service, as we helped build houses, feed homeless, work with those who were disabled, and served those who were in need. Unquestionably, it helped prepare me to become a foster parent, as Kelly and I opened our home to serve children who suffered.

The first five weeks of that year saw the cast members learning the songs, the dance routines, how to prepare the stage, lights, sound, and all that went into the two-hour performance. It was during the first week of staging where I first became aware of the Australian beauty. It was as if I was walloped with Cupid's own fist the first time I heard the striking young girl from the Land Down Under speak. Her Aussie accent was unlike anything I had heard before; when I heard her speak, it was as if the Angels from Heaven were singing in all their glory. Her voice dripped like a million ice-cream cones, much better than honey, and her smile was the prettiest thing I had perhaps ever come across. This girl, this Australian beauty, had me falling for her in a big way. I wanted to get to know her better right away. In fact, I needed to get to know her better. I was a desperate romantic, and my young lover's heart was calling out to this young lady.

"So, what do you look for in a boyfriend?" Kelly and I had been talking for a while now, and I was happy to be able to put this question to her. We were sitting at an event, listening to Rosa Parks speak, one of the pioneers in the American Civil Rights movement of the mid-20th century. I had maneuvered my way into sitting next to the one who made my heart do incredible feats of gymnastics, as my heart would jump, skip, and dance each time I saw her.

Without missing a beat, she replied, "Communication. It's important that a boyfriend be able to communicate, as well as be honest and open." She was a little taken back by the question, though, finding me a little forward. Perhaps it was how American guys acted, she thought.

If she found me a little forward at the Rosa Parks event, as it came to be known in our house, I clearly was forward in brazen fashion a few weeks later. The cast had completed staging, and had hit the road, with the first performance in Pasadena, California. The following day, my attempts at romance came to a screeching halt with the Australian.

Arriving in Placerville, California, the cast was met with something that most thought was very un-Californian; a snowstorm. Situated high in the California mountains, the town was smack dab in the midst of a snowstorm that would shut the city, and the performance, down. I soon saw an opportunity, though, to advance my cause, to woo the young Aussie princess.

As our cast was quite large, and there was a tremendous amount of stage equipment, show costumes, and a great deal of materials needed to make the year of traveling and performing a success, we traveled in four greyhound-sized buses, two 12-seat buses, and an 18-wheeler semi-truck. Arriving into any city was often an event, as a caravan of performers from around the globe frequently was the talk of the city, bringing out all forms of media, as well as a large gathering of people, including the host families that would take us into their home for the brief stay. However, the tremendous blanket of snow in this city altered plans for the host families, and altered my plans for romance, as well.

The blizzard had prevented many families from arriving to pick up their cast members, resulting in a bit of a panic. Some 165 Uppies had to go somewhere, yet not enough host families had arrived. The decision was made from management to find emergency host families for all of us. Any family that showed up and volunteered was good to go. Here was my chance: Carpe Diem was staring me in the face; it was time to seize the day. Grabbing my two suitcases, I rushed through the knee-deep snow over to Kelly, who was standing next to Tina, from Massachusetts. The two of them had found a host family. "Do you have room for one more?" I asked the family, putting on my best stage performance grin. A few minutes later, I placed my suitcases in the back of the vehicle, and headed off on the snowy road.

It was late that evening when I felt another cold front hit me. This one was the result of my own doings, though. As the home was without heat or electricity due to the power outage from the snow storm, we were lying under heavy blankets in front of the house's sole fireplace. Kelly and Tina lay in the sofa bed, while I was in a sleeping bag, on the floor nearest the fireplace. It was well past midnight, as the three of us were deep into discussion. The conversation took several paths that night. As we were all college student ages, it eventually led to romantic interests, and who each other was attracted to. When it was time for me to answer the question, I decided to risk it all.

"Well, there are a couple of girls I think are cute," I said. As the flames in the nearby fireplace were the only source of light, the two young ladies were unable to see neither the anticipation on my face, nor the slight case of nerves that creased my forehead. "Helene from Norway, Valerie from France, and Nina from Sweden are all cute," I expressed before pausing. I had grown to appreciate the importance of a dramatic pause, and felt this was an appropriate time to use one. With a smile on my lips that was hidden from the others from the lack of light, I delivered the exclamation point. "I also like Kelly from Australia."

"Me?" she asked, not expecting this full disclosure from some American she had only recently met.

"Yup," was my only response.

"Okay! I'm going to sleep!" Tina announced with great expression in her voice, as if this were a command for me to cease in my confession of love to the one who lay next to her. An awkward silence descended upon the dark room, as Kelly chose not to comment any further on the matter.

Though I did not possess the mastery detective skills of the legendary Sherlock Holmes, I was able to piece together Kelly's opinion on the matter through the clues she so cleverly dropped for me to find. She ignored me. Over the course of the next ten days, the young lady with the smile that would melt all the snow in my home in Michigan and the voice that had sent me in a state of near collapse ignored me. Apparently, my American charms had no effect upon the girl from Down Under. With my heart heavy, I soon focused my attentions on a girl from France, and shortly after that, to a girl from Sweden; both ignoring my appeals for love. My hopes for romance were a failure on more than one continent that year.

As the year progressed, Kelly finally did overcome her inability to talk to me, and we developed a deep and sincere friendship. So much so that we continued the friendship after the year of performing was over, despite all cast members going back to their respective homes and countries. Indeed, over the course of the next several years, we jetted back and forth between the two respective countries, wrote long letters, and spent large amounts of money on phone calls, all before the age of the internet, of emails, of video calls, and of texting. Yet, it was a very difficult relationship to be in the middle of, as the distance was so vast, and so very big. After a great amount of prayer, I knew the path to take was before me. In the summer of 1993, I decided to follow that path, where ever it might lead to, and whatever country it might lie in.

* * *

"Death to the Australian! Death to the Princess Kelly!"

It was June of 1993, and Kelly was being led through the large mall in my hometown of Battle Creek, Michigan. Just moments earlier, she had been eating lunch with my sister,

Karen, as the two of them were visiting for the first time since Kelly's return to the USA just three days earlier. It was during this meal when a costumed masked man, dressed as an executioner and holding a large plastic battle axe, came up to the two. After tying Kelly up with a rope, he paraded her through the mall for all to see, leading her to the center stage, all the while yelling his amusing death threats. As my friend Martin did so, dressed in the costume I had rented from the city's costume shop, the stores began to empty out, as many of the patrons and employees wished to see what all the commotion was about. Soon, the two reached the large entertainment stage situated in the middle of the mall. Tying her up in the chair seated directly in the middle of the stage, he continued with his ominous threats. The large crowd that had gathered was waiting for something to happen; anything to happen. It was my turn to act.

"I shall rescue the fair lady! I shall defend the honor of Princess Kelly of Australia!" Leaping from the nearby Sears store, I bounded through the mall towards the stage, dressed as the character Aladdin, from the recent Disney movie. With plastic sword in hand, I sprang up the stairs in my bare feet, and engaged the executioner in a duel, all the while shouting my love for the exquisite young lady. As she looked at me from her chair with an air of bemusement, the villain and I battled in a lengthy sword fight, each being struck with imaginary near death blows, over the course of the next five minutes. Finally, after slaying my adversary in dramatic fashion, I untied Kelly, releasing her from the chair. Kneeling down before her as she stood, I recited a poem her grandfather had written for her grandmother. Finishing this, I put forth to her the question all were waiting for.

"Will you do me the honor of marrying me?"

"Well, I don't know..."

This was, without a doubt, not the response I expected, and I reacted accordingly. I began to sweat. I sweated like never before. With my knees shaking, and my vision becoming a little hazy, I simply stood there, sweating as if I were the one waiting to be done in by the executioner standing behind me. By now, a large crowd had gathered from all parts of the mall, encircling the center stage many times over. Kelly's response drew mixed reactions. On one hand, there were a number of older ladies encouraging Kelly with "Yes! Yes! Yes!" This was great; this was the response I wanted.

Unfortunately, many of these older ladies with their encouragement of "Yes!" were drowned out by the even larger number of small boys, who found the entire event amusing, and decided to add to their amusement with their own voices. "No! No!" they shouted. "Don't do it! Don't marry him!" This only made me sweat all the more, if it were humanly possible. At this point, seeing that things were not going as planned, the masked executioner quietly and hastily walked off stage, perhaps to escape the carnage he was witnessing in this thorough breakdown of romance.

Watching the entire spectacle unfold before her, Kelly found this not only amusing herself, but also a little justified. Little did I know that Kelly had told her mother as she was about to board the airplane to the United States, "I think Boom's going to propose to me, Mom. I just hope he doesn't do it in a mall, in front of a large crowd." She knew me too well.

With the chorus of "Yes! Marry him!" and "No! Don't do it!" growing louder and louder, like dueling chants back and forth at a college basketball game, Kelly decided to end the agony that I was undergoing. Perhaps she didn't want to see the stage become a small pond from the sweat that surged from every pore of my body. With a laugh, she countered with "Oh, all right. I'll marry you."

Kelly had the audience cheering, with the exception of the boys in the front row who were now booing. She had upstaged me, the performer that I was, during my biggest moment, and I couldn't have been happier.

* * *

As often happens when children come into a marriage, the years flew by. We lived in Australia for a number of years, highlighted by the year living on Great Keppel Island, the tropical island located in the middle of the Great Barrier Reef, as we worked for the resort located on the tiny island. Nearly four years after our marriage, we moved back to the United States, and ended up in what we first came to believe was Mayberry, itself, from the popular television classic, *The Andy Griffith Show*. This Mayberry, though, was Monticello, a two traffic light town, where everyone knew everyone else, where many stores and the small town's two banks closed at noon on Wednesday, and church life dominated most people's life. It was idyllic for raising our three children, and we grew to love the town even as the town's people grew to embrace Kelly, the only Australian for miles and miles around. Indeed, despite my years on television, as I crisscrossed much of the South, working in the professional wrestling business from 1997 to 2000 as "The Professor," a manager for the so-called bad guys in the entertainment sport, I became the husband of the local celebrity from Down Under. Kelly's business as a massage therapist was more successful than either of us imagined, while my day job as an English and drama teacher was fulfilling in its own right. We were happy, and we were blessed. It was time, we both concluded, to share these blessings with others.

* * *

From the very first time a foster child entered our home, Kelly and I, along with our children, have been on a roller coaster of sorts. Sleepless nights, exhausted days, and emotionally heart-wrenching experiences were the norm. Neither of us had suspected the severity of this when we first signed up to welcome foster children into our home.

Both of us had felt led to foster at roughly the same time in our lives, as we wanted to help children in need in our community. After roughly a year of training, we took in our

first two children, four-year-old Mary Sue and her six-month-old sister, Sarah. The two had undergone some frightening experiences in their home before coming to us, experiences that Mary Sue would tell us in a disturbing fashion. At the time, our own children were quite young; Kolby was six, Jace five, and Brody only three. Though they only stayed with us for four months, they had come to be a special part of our family, leaving Kelly in grief when they moved out of our home, moving to live with their grandparents.

We were not alone for long, as Sydney came to live with us. The foster child, only seven years of age, was basically taking care of herself. Living with her severely alcoholic grandmother, the little girl had to find and prepare her own food each morning and evening, usually consisting of frozen hot dogs warmed in the microwave. Along with this, the parentless child, whose mother and father were both missing, was also responsible for getting herself ready for school each day. As a result, she often missed catching the bus each morning, and had a large amount of absences, resulting in her performing at a severely poor level academically. When the seven-year-old arrived in our home, she had very few academic skills, so much so that she could not even write her own name. Her behavior in school was also a challenge, often resulting in meetings between the school principal and myself.

Though Sydney's stay in our home was one filled with many challenges, she had become a valued member of our family during the year and a half she lived with us. Two days before Christmas one year, Sydney left our home and family and moved to the state of Florida, as her aunt and uncle had adopted her. I had great reservations and concern regarding this, as she had only met the couple one time beforehand. Despite my many pleas to the caseworker to have the young child stay with our family until after Christmas, Sydney instead went to live with the family she hardly knew, spending a Christmas with strangers instead of a family she had lived with and who had loved her for nearly 20 months. It was a

time of much sadness and tears in our home, as we all grieved the loss of this special child.

Many times, when a foster child leaves the home and is returned to a biological family member or parent, foster parents lose all contact with the child. For many birth parents and biological family members, foster parents are looked upon as the "bad guys," so to speak. There are those birth parents who feel that foster parents have taken their birth child away from them, or at least they place the blame upon the foster parents, in a bout of denial. This was the case with our family, as we seldom heard from the foster children that had come to live with us. For years, we heard nothing from Sydney, though we prayed for her frequently. Four years after she had moved from our home, we received a phone call from her one evening. Picking up the phone that evening, I was met with a familiar voice, asking "Is that you, Daddy?" Instantly recognizing her voice, I was thrilled to speak with her, and both Kelly and I were overjoyed to finally make contact with her. She had been placed into yet another foster home, this time in Alabama, after being bounced from home to home for two years. Sydney was taken from her aunt and uncle, who heavily abused her, and placed into several different homes the next several years. Speaking to her foster mother at the time of the call, Kelly had found that Sydney had run away from her foster home on occasion, had been in trouble a considerable amount, and had simply become difficult to live with. Both my wife and I were stunned that Sydney had called us, and had referred to us as the only "Mommy" and "Daddy" in her life. As we were traveling to Australia the next day for three weeks to visit Kelly's mother, we informed Sydney's foster mother that we would call her back when we returned.

Sadly, when we arrived back in the United States, Sydney had already been moved to a group home for foster children, a modern-day orphanage of sorts. The foster mother who had only weeks before taken Sydney into her home told Kelly upon our return that the now teenage girl had become so disruptive, so undisciplined that she was almost unadoptable. As she did not know the name or location of the group home our former daughter of 20 months had been placed in, we were unable to locate her. Despite attempts over and over again by both Kelly and I to locate Sydney, through searches on the internet, phone calls to various child welfare agencies in Alabama, and though our own connections here in Georgia, we met with failure after failure. To be sure, she would probably cause us a great deal of difficulties, but we felt strongly that we needed to contact her, to let her know that she was thought of, that she was loved, she mattered, and that she was still part of our family. Yet, Sydney was once again lost to us, leaving Kelly and I in grief, once more.

Many other children had come through our home, some staying as short as one day, like the four-year-old girl and her 18-month-old brother. The two had been found by the police, wandering along an interstate highway near our home. Other children came to live with us for four to six months, like Scotty, who arrived at the age of four. The boy was small in frame and only speaking two words, his constant battle cry of "Me hungry!" The boy endured severe neglect before arriving in our home, and suffered from the fact that all of his teeth had rotted out prior to living with us. Despite my protests of concern with the caseworker for his well-being and safety, the young boy went back to live with his mother, an environment I felt was not the best for him.

Four-year-old Espn and his four-month-old sister Melinda stayed with us for four months, as well. The two had been placed in our home due to the drug abuse of their mother, and the father was nowhere to be found. Espn had been horrifically abused by his mother, so much so that it continues to trouble both Kelly and me today. When Espn first came to our home, my wife discovered small, black, circular marks on his scalp. These marks were in fact burns, cigarette burns, from his mother. Frighteningly enough, the burns were not only on his scalp, covered by his blond hair, but on his tongue, the roof of his mouth, and even on his penis. His mother, the one person who was to love him the most, to protect him, and to guide him through life; the person who had given birth to him, had hurt him so terribly, had scarred him so appallingly, physically, emotionally, and mentally. Indeed, the young boy did not show any emotion while in our home, not joy, pain, sadness, curiosity, fear, or any other emotion. His young sister, a tiny baby, suffered from Meth addiction, and was our first excursion into that sad world. Their time with us was one of sadness and fatigue, as baby Melinda screamed day and night from her suffering from the complications of Meth. It was with some relief and joy that the two went to live with another foster family hoping to adopt the two.

Mariah was just five days old, and weighed just five pounds, when she came to live with us, spending her first four days in the hospital. As the tiny hospital in the small rural town we lived in did not regularly deliver babies, it was a surprise to many when Mariah was born in Monticello, instantly making news across the county. As her mother had been on drugs at the time, Mariah was placed into our care. Her first month saw the tiny baby suffer from the drugs in her body. Mariah was a Crack baby, and her tiny frame shook with the agony that gripped her body as she went through her own withdrawals. Watching her suffer each day and night filled me with not only sadness for her, but with an anger that I felt ashamed of. Once again, I was forced to watch a tiny child suffer from the actions of a parent, leaving me powerless to help.

Perhaps it was the fact that she came to us at only five days of age, perhaps it was due to her suffering, or perhaps it was due to her infectious smile that lit up the room—whatever the reason might be, all who came to know her fell for the tiny baby, with our own home coming to love her greatly. After 22 months as a foster child, and through many legal battles, court hearings, and countless calls to judges and attorneys as I fought for her, she formally became a permanent member of our family through adoption, with the name change from Mariah to Grace.

Not all adoptions through foster care are successful, though. Helena came to us with a story that was full of despair and sorrow. At age nine, her Romanian parents died, leaving her, her sister, and two brothers as orphans in the Eastern European nation. Shortly afterwards, she was adopted by an American family in New York, a family who promised to teach her English, to provide a safe home for her, and to love her unconditionally. After six months of heavy abuse, this family, who was to love her, instead gave her back to the state. A family from Pennsylvania then adopted her, promising to give her a house, a home, and a family that would love her. Yet, after one year of abuse, they too gave her back to the state, the second family "unadopting" her. Sadly, a third family in Georgia also adopted her, and abused her on and off for six years. One day, on her way to school, Helena was dropped off at the DFCS office in her city, as another family abandoned her, the third family to "unadopt" the Romanian-born child. At this point, she came to live in our home, a child who had been told that she would be loved, yet a child for whom the word "love" had become a word not to believe, not to trust.

Helena did not trust us when she first came to live in our home, and why should she have? We were strangers to her, another set of adults, another family who told her that we would care for her, we would provide for her, we would love her. Others had told her the same thing, yet had betrayed that trust, hurting her in several ways; ways I did not fully understand, nor probably wish to fully know. Though Helena instantly came to like Kelly, embracing my wife's warmth and pleasant personality, and interacted with our own children, as well as Mariah and Scotty, who were both placed in our home at the time, the 17-year-old struggled with our rules, our expectations, and our family values. It made for a tense home, and a stressful time.

Four months into her placement in our home, we received notification that all parental rights to Mariah were terminated, and that a search for any biological family members that might be fit to adopt her had ceased. This after a lengthy court battle, one that saw me testify in court against the baby's biological mother and grandmother, leaving all emotionally damaged. As Kelly and I began the process of adopting Mariah, I struggled with the fact that Helena had no family to call her own. "I want to offer her a place to call her own," I told my wife one evening. "When she's in college, where will she go for Christmas vacation, or for any vacation, for that matter? When she's married, where will she take her own children when she wants to take them to their grandparents for Christmas time? Who will she call upon if she has an emergency in the middle of the night?" I felt so bad for the Romanian, and did not wish to see her end up like so many other foster children who, after turning 18 years of age, "aged out" of the foster care system. The statistics were staggering for these lost young adults, these former foster children who made up 75 percent of the homeless across the USA, with 65 percent in prisons and jail cells, with many turning to drugs and early pregnancies. I wanted to offer Helena not only our last name, but a family for her future.

To Helena, though, "family" was a bad word, so to speak, and the unconditional love we offered her was one that was foreign to her, as well. She rejected both, and the adoption did not go through. She had had too many betrayals in her own life, and was simply waiting for us to do as so many others who had come before us had done. Indeed, the tension in the house rose to a level that became unbearable. Her behavior was one that was unacceptable in our home, and within our family, and we were forced to move her to a group home. The move left me ridden with guilt, as I was certain that I had failed her in some way, that there was something more I could have done to help her.

Over the course of the next several months, and into that next year, I wrote to Helena every other week, reminding her of our love for her, and for God's love for her, as well. I also encouraged her to continue in her school work, and filled her in on events in our own home. Kelly and I, along with our own children, traveled to the group home often, visiting with Helena, taking her out to dinner, and had her over to our house for weekends and holidays. Along with this, I helped her enroll into a nearby college, further encouraging her where others were not. As time passed, she grew to not only understand the concept of unconditional love, but also to accept ours. Though the adoption was never made official, she came to be an important member of our family, and like another daughter to Kelly and I.

Through the years, Kelly and I have taken a number of children into our home. To be sure, we were not experts in parenting, and had often made mistakes, both with our own children and with the many foster children who were placed in our care. We had also found that fostering was a difficult job, one that is exhausting, both emotionally and physically. Certainly, there were times when I did not enjoy being a foster parent. There were moments when I had become angry with birth parents, frustrated over the abuse and neglect that some had delivered to their own children. Many times during visitation days, days in which a foster child would spend a supervised visit with a birth parent or biological family member, the children would return to our home with broken promises by their birth parents of going back home or even false accusations made against Kelly and me. These were days in which the hard work the two of us had done with the children was often destroyed. The many restrictive rules and regulations that were placed upon foster parents by DFCS were also frustrating, as it made our difficult jobs all the more so.

In spite of all the heartbreaks, the exhaustion, the disappointments, and the frustrations, God's call in my life to take care of His children was a strong one, one that I could not ignore. The words of Matthew 25:35 rang true to me, speaking to my heart. "For I was hungry, and you gave me something to eat; I was thirsty, and you gave me something to drink; I was a stranger, and you took me in." There are so many hungry and thirsty children that need to be taken into a home, hungry for security and thirsty for love. There are those who say that fostering is not only hard work, it is also heart work; it truly is the hardest job I had ever grown to love.

Chapter 3

The Call came while I was at work one Friday. The Call was the phone call from DFCS, asking if we could take in a foster child. As usual, the Call took me by surprise, as they were always unexpected. Sometimes, Kelly would receive the Call while she was at work; other times, I might receive the Call while I was at work at the high school. There have been those times when the Call came while we were at home, or out for the evening with the children. Of course, there was the time, too, when Kelly and I were on our first date in well over a year when we received the Call to take in Scotty, the four-year-old boy who had suffered physical abuse from his father, severe malnutrition, and perhaps most disturbingly, all of his teeth had rotted out, leaving him with a mouth that was devoid of any teeth, whatsoever. Yet, in spite of this, his smile warmed the hearts of all who encountered him. Despite no teeth, Scotty's appetite was ravenous, spurred on by the only two words the four-year-old boy could speak when he came to our home. "Me hungry" was all he could utter, and he made it his battle cry, saying it to all he met. Scotty stayed with us for four months, and it was the first time we had seen our home bulge to six children, as Helena was with us, as well.

It had not even been two weeks since Linda, Joshua, and Micah had left our home, and we had not fully recovered over their loss. For many foster parents, grief is natural when a foster child leaves the home. After all, we had not only shared our homes with these three children, we had shared our lives and our hearts with each of them, as well, coming to love and care for each deeply. Watching children that we loved go back to an environment in which I feared would not be a healthy or a safe one was difficult and something that both Kelly and I struggled with. We were not only grieving, we were also exhausted. Yet, as I told Kelly many times beforehand, we were DeGarmos, we fostered; it was our call from God.

"Hey, John. It's Cathy from DFCS again. Hope I'm not bothering you," the caseworker said as I picked up the phone in my office. Cathy had called us four days earlier about taking in an 18-month-old baby, but the placement went to another family, as Kelly and I felt we were simply not ready for another baby, still grieving the loss of the other three only days beforehand. I always enjoyed talking to Cathy. After all, she enjoyed my jokes, and put up with a lot of my nonsense. Furthermore, I had spent the past few days feeling guilty for not taking in the baby, feeling that I had let Cathy down.

"Not at all, Cathy. How can I help you?" I asked, sitting down at my desk.

"Well, you told me to wait a few days…" she said with a nervous laugh—I could sense the anxiety in her voice—"… and it has been four days since I last called…" Despite her nervousness, I let out a deep laugh. Indeed, it had only been four days, and I did ask her to call me back after some time had passed since the three little ones had left our home. I guess this constituted a little time for DFCS caseworkers. Her next statement brought my laughter to a quick halt. "We have a family of five children who need a home, and…"

"*Five children?*" I interrupted her. I was stunned, nearly falling out of my chair. That would make nine children in my home. I was hardly prepared to take care of nine children. I had a hard enough time trying to stay above the waves with my own four. Nine would have me quickly drowning in a sea of children.

Cathy quickly responded, setting me straight. "Yes, but only three of them need a home, as two of the five are living in another foster home in a nearby county. Both parents are in rehab as they suffer from an addiction to Meth," she told me. Meth, Kelly and I had come to find, was quickly becoming a replacement for Crack, yet was so much more insidious, as it completely destroyed the lives of those who became addicted to it. The research that I had done on my own due to the Meth-related incidents with foster children in my home led me to find that the drug was relatively easy to make, as well as inexpensive. The most horrific aspect of it was that a user could become addicted by the first use. I had also discovered that the drug affected the brain so profoundly that it actually changed the way the brain thinks and acts, creating in it the need for the drug, the addiction aspect, to be at the same level as anything else the user needed to survive, such as air or food. Even more disturbing was the fact that the drug erases all forms of rational decision making, as well as the body's craving for food, or even sleep. As we had found with Linda and Melinda, babies born to Meth addicts faced a tremendous uphill battle for the rest of their lives. Without a doubt in my mind, I came to believe that Meth was a family destroyer.

"The boys are ten, nine, and seven years old," she continued, "and their four-year-old sister and three-month-old sister are already placed in the other home. Right now, the three boys are with that family, also, but we need to place them in another home, as that family can't take five children."

"How long will they be in custody?" I asked the caseworker.

"I don't know, John. If I were to guess, I would say they're going to be in care for a long time. Both parents have to go through rehab, and both might have to go to jail, as well. It could be a while. I know this is a lot, John, and I will sure understand if you say no."

I don't know what was louder: the sigh from the thought of seven children in the house again, or the laugh from the thought of the insanity of the possibility of taking these three boys in. "Well," I said, after both the sigh and laughter escaped my lips, "let me call Kelly first, please, so we can talk about it, and pray about it. Can I call you back, Cathy?"

"Of course, John, I understand. Let me know as soon as you can please."

After reassuring her I would, I immediately called Kelly. Fortunately, she was between clients, and had just a few minutes before she had to go in for her next massage. I quickly filled her in on all the details that Cathy had just given me only moments before. "What do you think?" she asked me.

"I don't know," I replied back. "It would be different this time, with these three, as they won't be in diapers." I laughed. "Plus, these are three boys about Brody's age, so he might have some playmates with him."

This time, it was Kelly's turn to sigh. "Let's pray about it," she said with some anxiety in her voice.

"Heavenly Father, we come to You wanting to do Your will. We thank You for the many times we have been able to take into our home Your children; children who are hurting and in need. We thank You for the many blessings You have given us, and continue to give us each day. We want to share Your blessings with others, and to serve You in all we do. Lord, You know how difficult this can be for us, and You know how wearing Micah, Joshua, and Linda were. Yet, we want to do what You would have us do. We look to You for guidance, and we ask that You show us what You would have us do. In Your name I pray. Amen."

As Kelly's time was quickly coming to an end on the phone with me, she simply asked, "So, are we crazy?"

"Yes, we are," I answered her.

"Does that mean we are going to do this?"

"I guess so, Sweetheart. It's what we do." I promised my wife I would find out all I could from Cathy, and then called the caseworker back. Finding out that the three boys would not arrive until after church on Sunday, I sat back in my chair, saying a silent prayer. Were we ready to take three boys in? More importantly, could we take care of three more boys? I wasn't sure, myself.

* * *

"Matt, Logan, and Derrick, this is Mr. John, and this is Miss Kelly. They are going to take care of you for a while." Kelly and I stood next to the caseworker that Sunday afternoon, greeting the boys. We had spent the previous day preparing for the boys' arrival. Only months before, we had converted our storage room into a nice guest room, complete with queen-sized bed, dresser, table, and chair. Realizing that our newest family members would not be able to fit into the room with this new furniture, I spent the day moving those out, and replacing them with a bunk bed, and another single bed, along with a book shelf. So much for our beautiful new guest room. I laughed to myself, realizing that the room never did get to host a guest.

As Kelly and I both introduced ourselves, I was immediately struck with how frightened the boys looked. Now, each time a foster child arrives to a foster home, it is always a new experience. We never know what to expect. Yet, there is always one constant; the children do not want to be in our home. After all, a child is taken from his mother and father, taken away from his family members, grandma, aunts and uncles, cousins. A child in foster care is also taken away from his friends, from his school and teachers, taken from his house and home. When a foster child is placed into another home, he is taken from everything and anything that is familiar to him, and is suddenly thrust into a strange person's home. The foster child doesn't know us. After all, foster parents are strangers. It is a strange home, full of strange people, strange rules, strange children, and strange customs. Everything about our home screams out to the children that they are not in their home. Of course the children are scared. Of course they are terrified. Why shouldn't they be?

What struck me about these three, though, was the level of fear in their eyes. Of the many foster children we had taken into our homes, these three showed a level of fear and anxiety that quickly pulled at my own heartstrings. My mind raced back to the very first night we had foster children placed in our home; four-year-old Patty Sue and her sister Sara. It was 10:30 at night when the two arrived, and Patty Sue was terrified. I had to scramble to lock all the doors in the house, while Kelly held the troubled girl close to her chest, as the little one continued to attempt to run out the doors, all the while screaming "I want my Mommy! I want my Mommy!" That was the first of many sleepless nights Kelly and I have encountered as foster parents, opening our eyes to the terrors that these children face each day.

As I quickly looked at the boys, each had a different look of fear in his face. The oldest, Matt, was trying his best to be brave for his other two brothers. The middle boy, Logan, had some anger in him, placing a very large emotional wall up in front of him, in an attempt to protect himself. The youngest was seven-year-old Derrick, and he was...well...seven years old. A little silly, yet still quite scared. All three stood huddled close together, and none of them would look either Kelly or me in the face. Fortunately, our own children once again stepped up to the plate, hitting a home run, as they introduced themselves to the boys, helping them to feel a little more at ease. I believe the addition of another boy their age, Brody, made a tremendous difference, as the boys seemed to be drawn to him. Nevertheless, it was three terrified boys who followed us into our home.

Taking the three black plastic bags in my hands that made up the small amount of their personal belongings, we showed them their new bedroom, and then introduced them to a plate of freshly baked chocolate chip cookies, in hopes that it might make the sudden transition in their lives a little more comfortable. Soon after this, and after a great deal of paperwork signing, the caseworker drove off, thus cutting off the last contact with the boys' family. Derrick quickly broke into tears, and Kelly rushed to embrace him, trying to comfort the little one.

After Kelly dried Derrick's tears, I tried a different route. I asked the three if they wanted to come along to church with me as I dropped off my three oldest children at youth group. With great hesitation, and a lot of encouragement from Kelly, the boys decided to come along. Throughout the entire two hours, the three boys stood glued next to me, never smiling, never speaking, and never engaging with children their own age. My own heart broke several times during those two hours, as I stood next to the three. For all my training as a foster parent, for all my experience during the past nine years, even for all my experience as a father of my own children, I was powerless to help these boys. There was nothing I could do to help ease their trauma, and it churned my stomach into knots.

When I arrived home, Kelly had sorted through their belongings in an effort to see what they needed. Each of the boys had only a few pieces of clothing in the black plastic bags, along with one pair of shoes. The clothes were tattered, ripped, and worn, and each reeked terribly of cigarette smoke, so much so that it was overwhelming. As we had done several times in the past when a foster child arrived in our home, Kelly washed the clothes several times in an attempt to rid the clothing of smoke. As it was late Sunday evening, we were unable to drive the 45-minute drive to the nearest clothes store, and decided to do it in the next few days. The boys were not only in desperate need for new clothes, shoes, and even jackets, they deserved them.

As we helped the boys get ready for showers for the older two and a bath for Derrick, I heard Kelly gasp slightly. "Boys, how long have you had those bites on you?" Silence reigned in the air, as no one spoke up. "Do those bites itch?" she asked.

"Yes, Ma'am," Matt answered, taking the lead as the oldest of the three.

"Okay. Matt, Honey, you get in the shower first, and Derrick, you come upstairs with me, Sweetheart, and have a bath. Logan, do you want to come upstairs and have something to eat?"

"No," he glumly said, with a frown covering his face.

"Well, that's okay, too. Why don't you just wait in your new room until your brother gets done with his shower, all right? Boomie, can you come and help me, please?" As I glanced over at her to reply, I noticed that she had a look of concern on her face, as her eyes were pleading with me to follow her up the stairs.

"Boom, I think they have scabies," she told me, in a hushed voice. "You're going to have to go into town and get some medicine for it."

"Scabies? What?" I was puzzled. "Never heard of it."

"Remember those times we had lice?" she quickly whispered to me, with a grimace. "It's kinda like that, only worse." As I got a jacket out of the closet, she hastily filled me in. We had battled lice several times with foster children, and I had discovered that treating lice was not on my top lists of favorite things to do. Lice, though, would have been a lot more fun, I later found out.

Like lice, scabies was another condition where the skin greatly itched due to a tiny bug or mite. Scabies, though, has the added distinction of having the tiny mite burrow under the skin. As it will not go away on its own, a special cream is used, I soon discovered, that is applied to the infected area. All three boys were suffering from the bites, as each of them had small red bites covering their bodies, with Matt suffering the worst. He was very much overweight, and his arms and face were covered with deep red scratches from the bites. All three boys were a mess. When I returned from the store, it was my job to cover the three boys with the cream. From head to toe, I painted their bodies white with the medicine that was to not only relieve them with their itching, but also a remedy to help combat the mites that were attacking their bodies. As I spread the scabies cream, each had a different reaction; Matt seemed embarrassed, perhaps due to his large weight, Logan would not allow me to spread the cream initially, but finally consented, and Derrick simply giggled throughout the process. His laughter was another form of medicine, and not just for the scabies.

As the night grew late, it was soon time for bed. Kelly read the boys a story while I cleaned up from the medicine on my hands and clothes. Joining her, we tucked each of the boys in bed, giving each a kiss on the forehead. We then went upstairs to attend to our own children, answering any questions they might have about their new foster siblings, and thanking them each for their help. If not for them, the day would have been much more difficult.

An hour later found me sitting in my library, lost in work on my doctoral dissertation. As I did, the sounds of crying wafted through from the nearby bedroom, instantly reminding me of the deep sadness that lay heavy in our house. Silently entering into the boy's room, I found Derrick sitting in his bed, with tears streaming down his face. Between heartbroken sobs, he asked me when he could go home. "I want muh Momma," he sobbed. "When kin I go home? I don't wann be here." Matt and Logan were asleep, or at least pretended to be.

Once again, all my training as a foster parent failed me, as I could not prevent this boy from experiencing the fear, grief, and sorrow that gripped his small body. Scooping him in my arms, I carried him to the library and sat down next to the pot-belly stove. What could I say to him to make him feel better? What could I do to take away his fear and sadness? My heart cried out to him, as I shared his own misery. This poor boy; this scared, lonely, poor boy. Once again, I felt the anger swell inside me; anger that parents could do this to a child, anger that those who were meant to love him the most had placed him in this situation with their own actions and their own choices. Saying a silent prayer to myself, I then stroked his hair. "I know, Derrick, I know," I whispered to him, wiping the tears that reddened his eyes.

"Kin we guh home tomorra?" he asked, his voice choking with emotion.

"I'm afraid not," I tenderly told him.

"When kin we guh home?" he next asked.

"I don't know, son."

His questions were emotionally difficult for me, as I grieved along with him. His next question, though, brought pain to my already anguished heart. "Don't muh parents love me any more?"

"Oh, Derrick, they love you very much!" I said, as tears began to swell in my own eyes. With a large lump in my throat, I choked the tears back before continuing. "They love you and your brothers deeply. You didn't do anything wrong, Sweetheart. They just have to work on a few things, first, and we are going to help them do that. Will you stay with us for a while, while your parents work on what they have to do?"

His voice broken by more sobs, he struggled to compose himself for an answer. "Okay," he replied weakly. Hugging him all the more tightly, I gave him one more kiss on the top of his head before taking him back to his bed. Placing the blanket over him, I crept out of the room, and headed upstairs to bed myself. Sleep did not come easy for either Kelly or I that night, though. Derrick was up two more times during the next few hours, his slight frame and little body shaking with more tears for his mother and father. Kelly took the midnight shift with him, while I went back down to him at three a.m. By the time morning had rolled around, sleep had pretty much escaped all three of us.

The next morning found yet another challenge for the boys, enrolling them in their new schools. Perhaps one of the most difficult trials a foster child confronts is that of public school. As I had found in my own research for my doctoral dissertation, the vast majority of foster children entered into care with learning disabilities of one nature or another. Indeed, many foster children have language delays, and poor reading and math skills, often due to the environment they came from. As foster children often are bounced from one home to another, many times the transcripts and school records of the child are missing when the foster child is enrolled in a new school. Yet, what is perhaps the most difficult challenge a foster child faces when being enrolled in a new school is the school environment itself. Everything about a new school reminds the child that he is, sadly, a foster child in a foster home. Whether it is a new teacher, new classmates, unfamiliar lunch room, getting lost in a hallway, or not taking the school bus back to his home, a new school is often the last place a foster child wants to be. During my studies, I clearly understood why foster children labored in school. Homework was last on their list of priorities, as they struggled with their emotions, trying to not only comprehend why they were in a new home, but also attempting to accept the fact that they would not be reunited with their parents any time soon.

Taking the morning off work, I enrolled Matt and Logan in their new school first. After filling out even more paperwork, I then walked each boy to his new classroom. Introducing myself to the teachers, I told each teacher as much as I could about the boys that I legally could, in an attempt to help the teacher better understand the boys' needs. I then quickly met with the school counselor and did the same. Unfortunately, we did not have any school records or transcripts from the previous schools, and did not know if the boys required any special educational needs or placement. I then rushed over to Derrick's new school, and did the same before heading off to work myself. As I sat down to begin work, I could not escape the image of each of the boys as he went to his new class, a look of despair and confusion; an image that haunted me the rest of the day, and long into another sleepless night.

* * *

"Hello Mr. John."

I turned around to see a boy standing in front of me, smiling. I had just entered into one of the few local restaurants in our tiny town to pick up dinner for the children on one of those rare occasions where we ate out. The restaurant had two other customers in it, besides the boy and me, an older-looking gentleman who I guessed to be in his mid-sixties, and a woman by the same appearance sitting at a table across from him.

"Hello," I said. I often found myself speaking to younger people that I did not know. Usually, these strangers who knew me, and knew me quite well, were former students of mine that I had taught through the years. This must be one of them, I thought to myself. "How are you doing?" I said, nonchalantly.

"You don't remember me, do you?" he said shyly, with a smile on either side of his lips. Perhaps I was too nonchalant in my response...

"Ummmm…" I began. I was racking my brain trying to find a name for this face. He clearly knew me, though for the life of me, I couldn't place him. By this time, the elderly couple was watching the conversation. I was stumbling and I felt it. My collar was growing too small; my forehead began to sweat a little. Was it getting hot in this restaurant? "I'm sorry," I said, as I meagerly grinned. "I don't remember who you are."

"I'm T.J. You were my foster parent for a few days."

T.J. Of course! T.J.! My mind quickly raced back to a few short years ago. T.J. had entered into our home just two days before his thirteenth birthday. He had been abandoned by his mother and found under an overhead bridge on a busy highway. Kelly and I were not in the habit of taking in foster children who were older than our own children, but felt led by prayer to do so on this occasion. We celebrated his birthday with breakfast in bed, gifts, cake, and a party, only to see him leave our home after three days to go and live with his grandparents. It was one of the few pleasant foster care placements that we had had, and we very much enjoyed T.J.'s short time with us. Now, here he was, standing in front of me. I rushed over to shake his hand.

"Hello!" My voice rang out in a shout. "It's great to see you, T.J. How are you? What are you doing here? Are you here long?" I was so overcome with surprise that I fired questions at him. It was great to see him, and my voice and face showed it, as I pumped his hand with a shake and a large grin enveloping my face. I soon found out that he was passing through town with his grandparents, who had adopted him. He told me how much he enjoyed his birthday with us, and even mentioned the skateboard that I had to chase all over a nearby city to buy him the night before his birthday. I introduced myself to his grandparents, and thanked them for taking him into their home. Though the visit with him was much too short, as I had to get back home, I told him how wonderful it was to see him, and that I would pass along his warm wishes to Kelly, before taking my leave. As I drove home, I thanked God for the visit with T.J. As difficult as fostering is, I needed a reminder of why we do it. T.J. had grown into a fine-looking young man, and was a testimony to the foster care system.

* * *

"You have *got* to be kidding me!"

Kelly's voice indicated that she was not in the most pleasant of moods. "What is it?" I shouted from the top of the stairs.

"The bathroom door...*again!*"

Oh no. This was not good. I rushed downstairs to see if my suspicions were true. To my dismay, I found that they were. Feces! Feces covering the downstairs bathroom wall and doorknob. Kelly's face told me she felt the same frustration, and disappointment, as I did.

Now, I had had my share of various forms, shapes, and functions that exit the body the past few years. I had caught vomit in my hand from a child, cleaned many an explosive diaper, and have had many a baby urinate on me. These were all welcome compared to chipping off the dried feces that caked the bathroom. This was the third time in the past several weeks that the incident, this natural disaster, had occurred. The first time, we found some in the garbage can, prompting me to sit the boys down and explain to them the relative importance of the proper use of a toilet. Apparently, from what we could gather from the caseworker, the boys had been raised in an environment where personal hygiene and toiletry skills were not as high on the list as on ours.

Yet, the feces were only the icing on the cake this time. When my foot left the last step down the stairs into the basement, the splash that I heard told me that things were not good in the DeGarmo household at that moment. There was a thin level of water covering the entire basement floor. When I reached the bathroom, I found that the toilet was clogged with a monstrous amount of toilet paper. In fact, from first glance, it seemed the entire roll had reeled itself in there.

I spent the rest of the afternoon cleaning the feces off the wall and, after calling a plumber to fix the toilet, mopping up the basement floor. While I attended to the clean-up patrol, Kelly had another talk with the boys about their hygiene and some basic toilet skills. During the month that the boys had come to live with us, we had come to care for them deeply. But what disturbed me was the fact that they had no basic eating, toilet, or social skills, as we had discovered. What kind of home had they grown up in, I wondered. More importantly, how could some parents treat their children in such a manner? The question was one I had no answers to, and that lack of answer troubled me greatly.

Chapter 4

God can move in incredible ways. Clearly, He had done so countless times in my life, though many times I simply was unable to see His hand moving until much time had passed afterwards. Without a doubt, my marriage to Kelly was perhaps the largest blessing I had received. Kelly's faith in God was a strong one, one that never wavered, even though mine did. Shortly after the death of our first born daughter from the disease Anencephaly, a condition where the brain fails to grow to its proper size, Kelly and I took two different paths in our grief. While Kelly relied on her faith to get her through that difficult time, I turned my back on God, and sought refuge in my work, as well as in my drive to work in the professional wrestling business.

After a while, I sought peace through other means, such as meditation and New Age forms of religion. Indeed, my anger towards God was so strong from the death of our first daughter, that when it came time to baptize Kolby two years later, I refused to do so in a church. Instead, the tiny two-week-old baby was baptized in the backyard bird bath behind Shirley's house, Kelly's mother, by a good friend of the family. I simply could not bring myself to step into a church, as I felt that God had rejected me. I, who had never taken alcohol, drugs nor smoked cigarettes, along with a wife who also had followed that lifestyle, saw the death of our first born from a disease that only struck one baby out of every one million babies. I found the irony of having this happen to Kelly and I while I watched others who did take drugs, who did smoke, and even those who did drink alcohol during pregnancy be graced with healthy children. This irony was too much for me, and I turned my back on God.

When it was time to move back to the United States, God's hand was surely in this, as well. My dream to work in the professional wrestling industry drove my every other thought during the first four years of our marriage. It was not only a dream; it was a passion of mine that bordered on obsession. I enjoyed the theatrics of the business, and wanted to work as a "Manager"—the individual who accompanied the "bad guy" to the ring, helped him cheat, and was basically in charge of getting the crowd to boo and hiss the "bad guy," while cheering on the "good guy." Though Kelly saw nothing at all redeeming in pro-wrestling, and in fact found it rather on the nauseating and repellent side, she encouraged me to pursue this childhood dream of mine nevertheless.

With this in mind, we left our island paradise in the Great Barrier Reef, and flew to the United States to chase this dream. Landing in a city and state that neither of us had been to before, we were soon in Atlanta, Georgia, the home of World Championship Wrestling. What struck many among our family, though, was that we moved across the world with a three-week-old baby, with no car, with no house, and with no job. All alone, in a strange city and, for Kelly, a strange country, with no means of supporting ourselves and a newborn baby. Yet, with God clearly in control and leading our path, we ended up in tiny, rural Monticello, where we quickly found a wonderful church family and a job for me teaching English and Drama in a nearby town. It was during this next year that I found my way back to God, restored my faith, and eventually began fostering with Kelly.

I have come to see that God has blessed our home many times the past several years as we fostered His children in need—whether it was with the adoption of Grace, the many meals that our church family had provided for us when new children came into the home, those times when we had others in the community provide clothes for new children, or the Christmases when our friends Lynne and Steve would act as foster grandparents for the children in our homes during those times, and provided all the gifts, making those Christmases a magical time for these children; some children who had never celebrated Christmas before, nor ever received a gift on Christmas Day, or even the excitement of Santa Claus visiting. To be sure, without the help of others, I don't believe that Kelly and I would have been able to continue fostering. At the very least, we certainly would not have been able to provide as much for the many children that had passed through our house as we had. Yet, God's hand was never so clear to me as it was than in the next few weeks to come.

For months now, Kelly and I had been planning a trip to Disney World for Spring Break. Our children suffered from the fact that my bride and I were bigger Disney fanatics than the average child. We enjoyed traveling to the parks any opportunity that we had, and had come to find the Magic Kingdom an escape from the exhausting pace that the two of us put ourselves through. After a very grueling past year with a number of foster children in the house, including the stressful and wearing four months with Micah, Joshua, and Linda, we were particularly looking forward to this trip. When we first booked the trip, the three had just left our home, and we were certainly not expecting another child so soon, let alone three. Nevertheless, the three boys did arrive, Disney was on the calendar, and we had a dilemma on our hands.

"Kelly, what are we going to do about Disney?" I asked her, one Sunday after church, after we had both arrived home. As was our custom, I drove the three boys, plus Brody, home in one car, while she drove our three girls in the other car. Once again, we were a two-car family, as we did not have a car big enough to fit all nine of us in.

"Well, it would be nice if we could take them with us," she said, as she changed out of her church clothes. "I hate the thought of putting them into respite for the week. It doesn't seem fair; they come to live with us, and then they go and stay with another family while we go to Disney World. Boomie, the thought of it is really a bit sad."

"I know, Kelly, but there is simply no way we can afford to bring them with us," I said. I, too, felt bad about the possibility of leaving them behind. "But, on the other hand," I countered, "it would be great if we could take them. You know, after all, they might never get the chance to go again. I don't imagine their parents will be taking them any time soon. Besides, what a great treat it would be for them."

Finishing up changing her clothes, Kelly sat on the bed, pausing before she went on. "It would be really hard, though, to take them. It would mean seven children at Disney, and we really wouldn't be able to relax." The disappointment in her face peeked through.

I laughed. "Yeah, you're right about that. And we would have to take two cars, which…I don't really want to do. The gas alone would be really expensive. I just don't see how we can do it."

"Well, it might help them adjust better here, and maybe help with the crying at night. If we took them with us, it might take their minds off their parents," my wife said. The boys had been with us for about a month and a half, and Derrick continued to cry himself to sleep. Along with this, Logan had begun to do so as well, though he would not allow Kelly or me to help him, his wall of anger and denial still in place. The boys had been having visitations with their father every two weeks, traveling the two-hour distance to the jail he was placed in. I had discovered that the father was in jail not only for manufacturing Meth in the home; he had also taken his three older boys with him to homes where he stole the copper from air conditioner units, and then sold the copper for money to support his own drug habit. The mother was in drug rehab, and was not allowed to have visitations for the first few months of her rehabilitation course. The boys did, though, receive a letter from her once a month. From the letters, it was clear that she loved her children. Yet, I could not get over the fact that the mother and father were both manufacturing drugs in the bedroom where the newborn baby slept, and that the boys were not even attending school when they were removed from their home, as we later found out. I was being judgmental; judging people whom I had never met, and I knew it was wrong. Still, I was angry that these boys had suffered so, that their parents cared more about their personal drug habits than the welfare of their children, and that they did not seem concerned about their children's education.

As a teacher, I knew fully how important a good education was to the future success of these children. Derrick's teacher had informed us that he was severely behind his other classmates, and that his reading skills were practically non-existent. As his school transcripts took almost a month to finally reach his new school, it was five weeks before he was able to be tested and placed into the appropriate programs that would help him. Kelly and I spent large amounts of time each evening helping him with his sight words, but he showed no progress. Logan was also behind in his reading. Even though he was in the third grade, he was reading at a first-grade level, and my wife and I were also working with him to improve this as well. Matt appeared quite intelligent, and his teacher told us that he was excelling in school. My concern, though, was that if he went back to his home, he would not get the proper support or encouragement he needed in order to be successful. I spoke to him on a regular basis about how bright he was, how well he could do in college, and the possibilities that lay before him. Indeed, college was a daily conversation we had, as I saw it as an avenue for him to escape his parents' own path.

Sitting down on the bed next to her, I took Kelly's hand in my own, asking her to pray with me. "Dear Lord, we look to You as the head of our household, and thank You for all the many blessings You have provided for us. Lord, we need Your help, and we look to You for guidance in this. We would like to take these boys to Disney with us, but we can't afford it.

Please let us know what You would have us do. In Your name we pray. Amen."

"Thanks, Honey," Kelly said before taking a deep breath. Exhaling it, she then said, "I don't think we should go if we can't take them with us. It's not what I want to do, of course, but it wouldn't be fair to the boys to place them in another foster home while we went on vacation."

Clicking my tongue in resignation, I agreed with her. "You're right. We probably shouldn't. It wouldn't be right. But I sure would like to go," I said, disappointedly. I was being selfish, and it bothered me.

The following day, I put in a call to the caseworker, Cathy, and asked her if there was any way we might get some financial aid for the children. I explained to her that we wanted to take the boys with us to Disney World. I told her how we felt that it might be a very special occasion for the three, and that it might help in their healing process. During the nine years we had fostered, we had never made such a request before, as this was a unique situation. I also let the caseworker know that we were not putting the boys in a foster home for respite care, but instead would simply cancel our trip if we could find no way to take the boys.

A week later, Kelly called me at work. Her excitement was evident as soon as I heard her voice on the other end of the phone. "Boomie, guess what?"

Now, for years, I had come to love this guessing game, no matter who I played it with. Here I was given three guesses, and I always enjoyed making the best of them. "Um…you have decided that you want to watch a Bela Lugosi film with me tonight." The 1930s and 1940s classic horror film star was my personal favorite.

"No, now let me…"

"You said guess what," I interrupted her. This was fun for me. "In 1846, your great-great-grandfather discovered a diamond mine, and you just got the letter saying you are the only heir to it."

"No! Now stop!" she commanded. She was not a fan of this game, and never really played properly. "Cathy from DFCS just left a message on my voicemail. She said that she was able to find a grant to take the boys with us. The money will cover about half of what we need. I know that isn't enough, but…"

"Wow!" This was something I never expected. In fact, I was counting on DFCS to say no to the possibility. Their funding had been cut drastically during the past few years, and I never imagined that they would be able to help in this situation. When Kelly and I first began fostering, there were a total of four caseworkers in our county. Now, due to budget cuts, there was one caseworker between four counties. As a result, Cathy was overworked, overwhelmed, and underpaid, like all child welfare workers in our state. "How did they get the money? I mean…this is incredible, Kelly!" I was simply astonished.

"Well, she said that she was able to find some money from a fund that was not being used at the time."

"That is so incredible, Kelly, but I still don't know if we can afford it. We have to pay for three sets of extra tickets, and a bigger room. Plus, the boys eat and eat, and we can't afford five days of extra meals for the boys, too. On top of that, what about the gas? We will have to take two cars down there and back, and the price of fuel for an extra car is not going to be cheap, either." I was being a little bit of a doom and gloomer, I felt, but at the same time, I was trying to be realistic.

"I know," she sighed. "I was just excited, and I want to go."

"I do too, Kel, and I think that is just wonderful what Cathy told you. I just don't know if we will be able to scrape the rest of the money together. That only really covers a little less than half of what we will need for the three boys. Let's just keep praying about it." She agreed with me before hanging up.

It wasn't a week later when Kelly informed me of yet another financial miracle showing me that God's hand was surely in this. A family of one of her massage clients had heard of our hope to take the boys to Disney World, and had graciously opened up their own wallets to help. Once again, we found ourselves in our bedroom, the only place a married couple could find to hold a private conversation. With seven children in the home, it seemed as if someone was always asking for something, crying about a perceived injury, hungry for food, or pestering another. Our bedroom was our Fortress of Solitude, or so I wished. There was always someone knocking on the door, it seemed. This time, it was Kolby, and we told her that we would be out in a minute. It appeared that no place was safe for us. Superman did not have these problems in his Fortress.

"We can't take this, Boomie. It's a check for a lot of money. It wouldn't be right..." Kelly told me, with a look of unease silhouetting her face.

"I understand," I reassured her, "but, Kelly, there are those families who feel that they cannot be foster parents, yet they want to help out foster children. This is how this family wants to help. They can't take these children to Disney World, they can't provide a home for them, but they can help the boys with this gift. This is a gift, Kelly. This is how they want to help. This is how they wish to serve God. Let them help," I pleaded with her. I, too, felt a little guilty about accepting the gift. Yet, I had come to accept a while back that there were those who could only help foster children with a monetary gift. This was a blessing not only from the family, but from God, as well. With this, we would be able to go.

Kelly soon relented. "You're right," she said. "Besides, God has provided just the right amount of money we need. He knew exactly what we needed to go; it is a blessing."

With the two of us in agreement, we began to make plans for going. The first thing we wanted to do was tell the boys. The two of us were anxious to see their reactions. After all, this was to be their first trip to the Magic Kingdom, to see Mickey, Donald, Goofy, and their friends. It was their first chance to ride down Space Mountain and explore the Haunted House. Kelly and I were excited for them.

Calling them into the kitchen, we sat down at the table. "Boys, we have a surprise for you," Kelly began. "Would you like to take a trip during Spring Break?"

"Um…I duh know." Matt was the only one to give a response. The anticipation was not building as I expected. I decided to take another route, and just spring it on them.

"Boys, we're going to Disney World!"

With one voice, the boys erupted into cheers, each falling out of their chairs. While hugging us in joyous laughter, they commented that it was the greatest gift ever. It was a dream-like response for all involved.

Indeed, it was a dream, because that is not what happened, for the actual response was nothing like that at all. Instead, their reaction was one neither Kelly nor I predicted. Instead of peals of laughter and happiness, there was a very un-Disney-like response. There was crying. Derrick and Logan began crying. Who cries about Disney World, I thought. Matt simply stood there, silently looking down at the floor. As the crying began to increase in volume, it was apparent that the situation was growing out of our control.

"Boys, what's the matter?" Kelly asked, taken aback by the reaction in front of her. In an attempt to comfort Logan, she tried to soothe him by placing her arm around his shoulder. I found the whole situation puzzling; who needs to be comforted when going to the Magic Kingdom?

It took Kelly and me a few moments to bring some calm to what was quickly becoming the Mickey Mouse Mountain of Misery. When we did, Kelly once again asked the boys what the problem was. Wiping his face with his sleeve, Derrick was first to speak. "Can our Mommy come wit us?" His Southern accent was thickened with emotion.

"I'm afraid not, Sweetheart," my wife gently told him.

Logan was next, asking "How long wilt we be gone fer?"

"We'll leave that Friday after school, and come back the following Saturday," I reassured him.

With a puzzled look, Kelly asked, "Boys, don't you want to go?"

Matt continued to remain silent in the Disney Dilemma, and Logan joined him. Derrick uttered what was perhaps on all of their minds, giving Kelly and me a little insight into their fears. "Will it mean we can't not eveh go back home agin?" With this, his crying resumed, fresh tears mixing with the ones that had previously reddened his face.

"Oh, Honey, it doesn't mean that at all," she replied, her own Australian accent stronger from the emotions swirling inside of her.

"Yes, boys," I added, "it has nothing to do with not going home. We just want to take you on a trip to Disney World with us. It's a great place, and when we are done, we will come back here. Kolby, Jace, Brody, and Grace have all gone lots of times, and will go this time, as well. I think, boys, that you will really enjoy it. It's one of Miss Kelly's and my favorite places, and we really would love to share it with you."

"Okay..." Matt and Derrick both murmured. Logan only nodded his head, yes, wiping his own tears from his face. The rest of the evening saw Kelly and I tell the boys about some of the wonders they would see, the attractions they could ride on, and the fireworks they would witness. By the time we lay our heads on our pillows, we were emotionally exhausted ourselves. Yet, little did we know that we had much more to be exhausted with on this trip.

* * *

Our small caravan of two cars pulled out of the driveway shortly after school was out that Friday. Kelly was in one car with our three daughters, while Brody and the three other boys were in the other car with me. How the Brady Bunch ever did it, ever traveled together, was beyond me.

Cathy met us in our driveway, delivering the paperwork that was needed in order to take the three boys over state lines. As foster parents, we needed permission to take any foster child on a vacation, and in this case, the boys' parents had to agree for the boys to travel outside of Georgia. Indeed, the mother sent a note saying that she was grateful for us taking her three oldest children.

Earlier in the day, I had to check Derrick out of school and bring him home with me, as he was complaining about an illness in his stomach, running a small fever in the process. As we began our seven-hour road trip, Brody also commenced to speak of his own stomach pains. I suddenly began to be fearful for my own well-being; not for falling ill, but for embarking on a journey that could be very unpleasant. Fortunately, though, there were no incidents, domestic or international, and the long trip was uneventful. It was close to midnight when we arrived, and Kelly and I dragged seven very tired children into our large hotel room.

The following day began our five-day expedition into the multitude of vacationers in the Magic Kingdom. The park was crowded, as usual, and Kelly and I were diligent in monitoring our troop. With my wife in front, and the children straggling loosely behind her, I followed, constantly keeping track of each child. Pointing at each child's head, I counted aloud to myself, "One, two, three, four, five, six, seven…one, two, three, four, five, six, seven," time after time, hour after hour, and day after day. I had no strong desire to lose a foster child, let alone one of my own children, on this trip.

The trip was an exhausting one for Kelly and me. While all seven children had a great time, we had felt the stress of taking care of and looking after so many children. Whereas our own four were pros by now with Disney, and acted accordingly, the three boys were a tornado of action, whipping in and out of lines, hollering in the hotel, running around the large pool, and generally creating a cyclone of motion and clamor. In other words, they had the time of their lives, laughing and playing like happy children should. With the money left over from those who so graciously donated, we were able to buy the children a shirt and hat each, as well as some ice cream and other treats at the various Disney parks. The trip was truly one that was most therapeutic for the boys, as they were able to put their own fears and concerns aside for the week. In truth, it was a bonding experience for our entire family, all nine of us, and even helped to break down the walls of anger and denial that Logan held so strong before him. Derrick's own giggling during the trip brought all of us to laughter many a time.

The caravan arrived home Saturday afternoon, and with it were nine very weary and exhausted travelers. It was Easter Saturday, and Kelly and I had our work cut out for us in order to make it a memorable Easter Sunday. Easter is a special time in our home, yet this year was especially so. Once again, God's blessings upon our household were very evident during this time of His resurrection. In fact, this time of new birth and renewal turned out to be one that would renew my hopes and faith once again.

The family that had so graciously helped us with Disney, allowing us to take the boys for the trip of their lives, had also graced us with yet another gift. This family, whom I did not know, whom I had never met, and whom had never met the three boys, was so touched by Kelly's own living testimony of her faith and her service to foster children that they not only wanted to help out with the vacation, they also wanted to do something for Easter, as well. We were given the gift of Easter baskets for each of the seven children in the home, as well as an Easter dinner provided for us. It was clear to me, God's hand was surely at work, and we were being showered with His love.

Returning to work that Monday morning, my cup was filled, so to speak, and I felt so very refreshed. Though the trip was a draining one, Kelly and I both felt rejuvenated; our foster parent batteries were recharged, giving us the energy to plough forward through each day's challenges. I felt great, and there was nothing that was going to change my spirit. Yet, the first email I opened up at work that morning soon saw much of my exhilaration fade away into grief.

I received an email from a former colleague of mine at my previous job, English and drama teacher at a high school in a nearby county. He told me of a foster child that had been placed into a home in his area. The child, only five months of age, was in a full body cast, as many of the infant boy's bones were broken. In his rage and fury, the birth father had repeatedly slammed his tiny son's body against a bed post, crushing his small bones. Furthermore, the child had human teeth marks throughout the body, as the father would bite down upon the child in his own anger. When I read of this, my own eyes saw red, as I became outraged over the condition of this tiny little baby, a baby who was unable to defend himself, whose only crime lay in the fact that he was born into a family that was not prepared to care for him, nor love him. Images of a baby being slammed repeatedly against a bedpost troubled my mind, as my heart went out to this helpless baby.

Yet, what was even more disturbing to me was what I read next. My friend went on to inform me that the biological parents of this baby were both recent students of mine. Students of mine! The fact of this hit me hard, and left me trembling in my chair. I had been their teacher, and an example to them on a daily basis. I had been a witness to them and a model. Or so I had first thought. Now, with the horror of this news, I felt that I had failed them. I had failed in being enough of a positive role model for these two students, enough of one to prevent this shocking and horrendous crime from being committed. Surely, I thought, there was something more I could have done as their teacher, words I could have spoken that would have prevented this atrocity. I had let them down, but more importantly, my failure had brought such pain and suffering to this tiny baby; this baby who had been beaten so severely, who had experienced such pain in his brief life. Placing my head in my hands, the grief overwhelmed me, and I began to weep.

Chapter 5

Spring was in full bloom. I believe the season was my favorite time of year. As a gardener, I relished the opportunity to dig my hands in the cool soil and plant flowers, prune bushes, and prepare veggie beds. Our six acres reflected my love of gardening, as the one thousand plus daffodils I had planted through the years were in full bloom. The birds were nesting in the budding trees, and the butterflies were beginning to gather around the dozen or so butterfly bushes planted throughout our yard. I found that I could not be outside enough during this time of year, and I encouraged the children to help. For Matt, Logan, and Derrick, it was a time of learning, as the boys had never experienced a garden or flower beds before, and our yard had plenty to offer, with over an acre of flowers alone. They also found great pleasure with the pet rabbits, turkeys, and ducks living on our tiny farm. Collecting eggs from the chickens was also a new joy for the boys. I was pleased to see that Kelly's and my hope of animal therapy was working with these three, as it had for numerous foster children that had come to live with us through the years. Indeed, the boys were starting to feel more relaxed, and more "at home."

With the advent of Spring, another school year was beginning to wind down. For a number of years now, the principal at the high school had been asking me to help with a fundraiser. Now, I don't mind helping with fundraisers. As a teacher, and as a parent, I recognized the need to raise money for school activities, as well as for opportunities for the children. Without the additional money raised from these fundraisers, there would be many lost opportunities for not only my own children, but for many children in the community. Nonetheless, the fundraiser he proposed was a bit different than the others, and was, unfortunately for me, one that only I could help him with. After years of resisting his pleas for help, I finally consented. Professional wrestling was about to invade small-town Monticello.

The big night came. The ring was set up in the middle of the school's gymnasium, and the pro-wrestlers were in the back locker rooms, getting ready for the night's action. I wandered back stage, and found that there were few faces I recognized from my own time in the business, as ten years had passed since I last stepped foot into the squared circle, as the wrestling ring is known. The promoter of the show was also a wrestler, and was a former student of mine years back. He had been insisting for some time that I come back to the business, and jumped at the chance of putting on a show in my town. He contacted the wrestlers, brought the ring, published the posters, and did all the little things that this small-time pro-wrestling organization needed to do.

Kelly and I, along with the seven children, all sat in the front row, with many of our friends, neighbors, and fellow church members filling the chairs and stands around us. Before the first match started, my former student, Chris, known as The Ticking Time Bomb, came out and heckled me before the crowd, calling me out as the former "Professor," and said I was a washed-up manager. He even had with him my old hollowed-out dictionary, which I had lent him when I first arrived. The dictionary was used to conceal brass knuckles, a chain, white powder used to "blind" the opponent by throwing it in his eyes, or anything else I might need in order to "cheat." With my own children looking on, and with the crowd behind me encouraging me to respond, I simply sat there, with a smile across my face, reminiscing in the entire atmosphere of it.

Finally, it came time for the main event. The two "good guys" were friends of mine that I had worked with all those years ago, and they were battling the evil fiends of the Time Bomb and his malevolent partner. Throughout the match, Mr. Bomb continued to harass me, and, at one point, spit water from his mouth onto me, in hopes of humiliating me. My children, along with the three boys, were not sure how to take it, as they had never seen their father in this position before. Indeed, Grace was in near tears, and huddled close to Kelly. With the crowd chanting for me to respond, and the heckling and harassment at a fever pitch, I picked up the dictionary, and swung it full force upon the Ticking One's head, landing a blow that "knocked him out." As the "good guys" rolled him up for a pin, the crowd erupted into spontaneous applause, with my wife laughing in the process. The night was fun for all, money was raised, and I was able to close one chapter in my life with a proper goodbye, something I did not do years ago when I first walked away from it.

* * *

"Whose shoe is that on the roof?" All seven of the children were standing in the front yard, pointing up to our green metal roof. For some reason, there was a white tennis shoe midway up it. Meeting only silence, I asked again, "Whose shoe is that?" At this point, Grace ran into the house, the pressure too much for the four-year-old to handle.

"Derrick's." His oldest brother paused before answering my question.

Confused, I then put forth the question that would logically come next. "Why?"

"I dunno," the seven-year-old responded. If I was looking for logic, I had better go inside the house and speak to my wife, I quickly determined, because there wasn't any around me at the moment.

"We were playing, and he threw it up there," Logan put forth.

Still not finding the reason behind this curious action, I tried once again. "Derrick, why did you throw your shoe up on the roof, Sweetheart?"

His eyes met mine before finding the partial green grass from the warming spring weather. Studying the ground before him, it was evident that he was searching for the right answer. I waited, patiently, for what I felt would be a valid and reasonable explanation, one that would bring rationalization into this most curious of circumstances. After a moment of analysis and personal reflection, he sallied forth with an answer that gave clarification and enlightenment to this quandary we were now facing. Looking up, with poise and self-assurance, he firmly and confidentially explained his actions. "I dunno."

"Ah," I said, shaking my head in understanding, "I see." The next hour saw the four boys and the two older girls watch me as I tried to get the shoe down by a variety of methods. As the roof was too steep for me to climb on, I tried a broom and then a rake, in an attempt to drag it down while standing on the ladder. When this failed, I then threw up a basketball at the shoe, hoping the ball would roll the shoe down. Following this fruitless endeavor, I then threw a football at it, optimistically hoping that would bring it down. While I had been cheered on at first, I noticed that my audience had slowly dwindled back inside throughout the hour-long attempt. Finally, only Derrick remained. "Well, Derrick," I said, patting him on the head, "it looks like we just might have to get you some new shoes." The downcast look that was on his face throughout the failed Shoe Rescue was replaced by a beaming smile, making the entire lost undertaking worth it.

This was the second year I had been conducting the children's choir at our church, and the boys seemed to enjoy it, practicing with Kolby, Brody, Jace, and the other children. Following the Sunday practice each week, the boys joined the others for a two-hour youth group session, which included dinner, games, and a light bible devotional or study. For a number of years, children of the church spent a week at a music camp. For the past couple of summers, I had served as a counselor and drama teacher for these week-long camps. I had enjoyed watching Kolby, Jace, and Brody learn music, theatre, and arts and crafts, all the while being enveloped in a Christian environment. This coming summer, I was hoping that Matt, Logan, and Derrick would be able to join the others for this week-long adventure, and Kelly and I began to put some money aside for them, counting on DFCS to help as well. The camp would benefit the three in a number of ways, I felt, opening them up to new experiences, traveling to another part of the state, and surrounding them with children their own age who were also separated from their families, albeit only for a week.

The boys had continued their visits with their father, traveling every two weeks after school to the prison he was incarcerated in. It was during the third month when they began visiting their mother on Saturdays, who was still in rehab, though now she was allowed visitors. The visitations were still difficult for the three, as they would come home with many questions, yet the tears had mostly dried by this time, though Derrick still had some nights where he cried himself to sleep. To be sure, it was difficult for not only the boys, but for Kelly and I as well. The boys looked forward to the visits, yet always came home brokenhearted, missing their parents dearly. It was these evenings when my wife and I had to pick up the pieces, so to speak, as the boys would often show their sadness by misbehaving, being lethargic, or through some other means that would necessitate both of us to show even greater patience with the boys, extra hugs, more affirmation, and larger doses of unconditional love.

Sadly, Logan's reading did not show signs of advancement with his school work and reading skills, though we helped him with his reading each evening after school. Derrick, also, did not progress in his sight words and basic vocabulary, either. In fact, it seemed like there were those evenings when we were going backwards. The youngest of the trio had a list of basic words he was to learn; words such as "the," "of," "is," "in," "and," and so forth. There were those evenings when he would be able to read some of them, while there were other evenings when the words seemed completely foreign to him. Fortunately, he was now getting the help at school that he so desperately needed, help that was not shown him in his previous school, we were told. I worried about both boys, concerned that they would fall behind even more, if not in the right environment. I was also troubled about Matt. Though he was succeeding in school, and had performed at a high level academically, my doctoral studies and research had shown that many foster children dropped out of school, and the percentage of those who went on to college was alarmingly low. I shared these concerns with the new caseworker assigned to the boys, as Cathy had taken a promotion, and was now working in a regional office for DFCS.

Both Logan and Derrick's school challenges reminded me of Sydney's own struggles. The former foster child of ours, like so many other foster children across the nation, struggled mightily with her school work. So many times, when a foster child is placed into a new home, the child is already behind academically. Compound this problem with the fact that when a foster child enrolls in a new school, the child is faced with the dilemma of missing transcripts, missing school records, grades, information, etc. With this information missing, it is difficult for foster children to be placed in the appropriate classes; classes which often are needed to properly help them in any special educational needs they might need. Along with this, new schools do not have important behavior and background information that might be needed to better understand the child's actions and needs. To further complicate this, most foster children have poor reading and math skills. When records and transcripts are missing, schools are unable to properly test these children for special assistance. Sydney suffered from a variety of these issues; poor math skills, poor reading skills, terrible behavior.

Logan and Derrick also suffered from poor reading and math, and we saw little sign of improvement in our home, though we worked with them nightly, as well as worked alongside their teachers in an attempt to best aid them. Fortunately for us, both of their teachers were fellow church members with Kelly and me. Lauri, with two young children of her own, was Derrick's teacher, and he was enamored with her. Amanda, who was pregnant with her first child, was Logan's teacher, and she developed many strategies designed to help him. It was sad watching these two struggle, and I was very concerned for their future. These two boys needed full-time attention from parental figures at home, each evening, after school, if they were to succeed. If not, their future did not look so bright regarding school and future careers, I worried.

* * *

For some time now, Kelly and I had been planning a trip to Europe to visit some of our Up With People friends, or Uppies, as we referred to ourselves. The previous summer, both my wife and I had the time of our lives, recharging our batteries, visiting with dear friends whom we traveled the world with, and watching the years disappear, as we joined other Uppies in Arizona for a reunion. Kelly and I were so transformed by that gathering that we wanted to do it again, this time with our European friends, most of whom we had not seen since we traveled together 20 years prior. We began plans for it the past July, shortly after we returned from the Arizona event. At that time, we had no foster children living with us. Yet, life as a foster parent often meant a life of flexibility, changes, and curveballs. Though we were taking our own four children with us on the European encounter, we were not prepared to take the three boys with us. Besides that, we would not have permission to take foster children out of the country, as it was difficult even taking them out of the state. As our June trip loomed closer and closer, we began planning for respite for the boys. Who would take them for the three weeks we were scheduled to be away?

It was a problem that we did not have to face. We received a call in late May that the three boys were to move in with their grandparents after school was out for the summer. Though Kelly and I had no plans to adopt the boys, I did not wish to see them go. We had grown very fond of the boys, coming to love each in a different and special way. Along with this, Brody was to lose his comrades in arms, his soldiers of fortune, his fellow superhero squadron members. My son had been surrounded by girls his entire life, with not only his own sisters, but a host of foster sisters marching in and out of his home. Dresses, high heels, and baby dolls often littered our floors, while Brody had a small area carved out for him with Legos, trucks, and action figures. The only boys who had come to live with us were either in our home for either a matter of days, like T.J., or much too young for him to play with, like Scotty and Espn. Matt, Derrick, and Logan were all around his age, and all three idealized Brody. He was the leader of the pack, enjoying himself running through the woods, making secret hideouts in the forest, playing in his tree house, and playing with them in the swimming pool. My son's four-month life in Never Never Land was about to end. More importantly, Matt, Logan, and Derrick were to be returned to an environment that deeply troubled me.

"I don't know," I said to the caseworker, Anne, over the phone one day in late May. "I'm just concerned for their well-being, for their welfare. I know, I know, I'm that foster parent that you just don't like to hear from," I told her, "but I care about these three boys, and I am going to fight for them and their future."

"I understand, John," Anne responded, "and we are doing all we can for them. They need to be with their family."

"I appreciate this, but I wonder if this is the best place for the children. After all, they were living with their grandparents when their parents were caught with the drugs, with Meth, in the babies' own bedroom. As you told me a few times in the past, both of the sons of the boys' grandparents are in jail; both of them. This just doesn't look like a good track record. Besides," I continued, "the grandfather is away working all the time, and the grandmother had a stroke recently, and can't even lift up the baby sister, let alone help the boys around the house. How is she going to be able to help the boys with their school work, when she, herself, has to be helped? Again, I just don't see how this house is a better environment than our own. Along with this, Kelly and I both understand the importance of a strong education. These three boys have missed so many days of school already, and were not being forced to go each day. Or am I mistaken? Can the grandparents offer the boys more than Kelly and I can? Are the three better off with the grandparents?" I was upset, and I was being judgmental once again to people I had not met. Still, I had grown to love these boys, and I was fighting for their futures. If I did not, who would, I thought to myself. I did not want a similar fate for Matt, Logan, and Derrick as I watched with Sydney.

"I know how you feel," the caseworker told me, "and we will work with the grandparents. We will tell them how important school is, and see that the boys get some tutoring help, if they need it. But, John, you aren't planning on adopting them, so you need to just let it go. They can't stay with you forever." She was right; I did need to let it go, though it was difficult. She was also right in that I had no plans to adopt the three, a thought that had never entered my brain. There was simply no way I was equipped to take in three more people into my home. Adoption was a process that I had no plans on visiting ever again in my life. I had four children; Helena made five. Five was plenty, good and plenty. But, it was difficult to let this argument go; I worried about the three. I worried about their school, their health, their safety, and their future.

After the conversation ended with Anne, I hung up the phone, sighing heavily. My stomach was in knots, with the tension in my neck shooting pain through my head and jaw. The stress of the situation was causing me much discomfort, and I tried to relax. I could hear my wife's words in my head, though, knowing her response would simply be, "Give it to God." I tried to give it over to Him, letting God be in total control. After all, this was out of my hands; I had done all I could for the boys' well-being. One of the most difficult parts of being a foster parent was letting them go. When we took these three in, as we did all foster children, we knew from the moment they entered our home that there would be a time when they would leave us. For Kelly, the hardest part was the grief over their departure, the loss of loved ones in the home. My biggest challenge was watching children go back to an environment that was not a healthy one, and sometimes not a safe one.

In this case, while the grandparents probably loved their grandchildren very much, I struggled with the doubt that love would not be enough for these three. Logan and Derrick needed daily help with school work, with their reading and math skills. Matt, with his intelligence, needed someone that would not only encourage him in school, but someone who would help him make the right decisions that would lead to college. Frustrated, I did not see any of these avenues as possibilities for the boys. The frustration I felt in the child welfare system, though, was my own failing, as I was not able to be in control. Once again, I felt I had let children under my care down, adding to my frustration. My wife was right; I had to give this over to God, trusting in Him. Yet, I found this hard to do, despite a great deal of prayer.

The following day, Kelly and I sat the boys down and informed them that they would be leaving. Like most foster children, they were excited to go and live with their grandparents, as it was their family. Sadly, in our foster parent training, we had discovered that most foster children wanted to go back home, even those who had suffered from physical and sexual abuse. There were exceptions, of course. Thus, it was no surprise that Matt, Logan, and Derrick wanted to move to their grandparents, as they had not been abused in this matter. Nevertheless, I was concerned. I did not share these concerns with them, or my own children, simply confiding instead with my wife. The boys were to remain with us for one more week, this last week of school before summer vacation. I still felt that the music camp would be beneficial to them, and reassured them that they could still go. Logan and Derrick showed no interest, though Matt said he would still enjoy going.

The next week was spent preparing for them to leave. We made sure all of their school records were complete and ready to go with Anne. I shared with her the concerns of both Logan's and Derrick's teachers, along with the information regarding any special services that they benefitted from while in school. All of their clothes were packed, along with their other belongings. During their four-month stay, they had accumulated a great deal, from books, clothes, and toys to other items. Kelly and I had to buy each of them separate large plastic containers for each, along with the suitcases that were provided them from our foster parent association. Members of our church also said their goodbyes to the three brothers that final Sunday.

It was Thursday evening when we packed the boys up in the car. Though the next day would be the last day of school, Kelly and I, along with the caseworker, had determined that this day would be best to take them to their grandparents. Friday would be so very hectic, as we were leaving for Europe early Saturday morning, and would not be able to truly give the boys the proper and loving send-off they dearly deserved while in the midst of preparing for the overseas trip. This time, it was my turn to watch this group of children leave while standing in the driveway, just as Kelly had months back when Micah, Linda, and Joshua left. Giving each boy a final hug, I reaffirmed my love for them through the tears that threatened to rain down my cheeks. As the weather that evening promised a storm, Kelly was anxious to get on the road for the trip. Keeping her company through the sad ordeal was Jace, while Kolby, Brody, Grace, and I stood waving, with the three returning our waves, with tears of their own. Matt's tears had surprised me the most, as they were the first ones he had allowed in our home over the past four months.

I was in the kitchen, folding laundry, when Kelly and Jace walked up the stairs. It was late, and I thanked Jace for helping her mother before kissing her goodnight. The others were already in bed for the night, and I wasn't too far behind them. Yet, I was anxious to hear from my wife about the boys.

"Boomie, it was an awful drive home. The storm was so strong, and it rained so hard, that I couldn't see where I was going. Jace and I had to pull over to the side of the road for a while because the wind was pushing our car around. It was awful!" My wife was shaking from the memory of it, and I quickly enveloped her in a hug. Eight years ago, she suffered from a frightening car accident when the car she was driving had a tire blow, her car careening off the side of the road before striking a tree. Her head went through the driver's side window, leaving her a bloody mess, glass stuck in her face and head. Since that time, I always worried for her safety when she drove at night. As I held her in my arms this time, I thanked God in prayer for bringing her home safe. After a few moments, my wife continued.

"The drive there, though, wasn't bad, as the ride was sad and beautiful at the same time," Kelly told me, as we both sat down in the lounge room. Her own sadness shone in her eyes, and it was evident that she had been doing a great deal of crying herself. "The grandmother met us at the front door. She couldn't help us with the boy's belongings, because of her stroke. She was so happy to see us, and had the house so very clean. It was obvious she had spent a lot of time preparing for them, and had done all she was supposed to do from DFCS in order to get the boys back."

"Was the grandfather there?" I asked, trying to picture the reunion in my own head.

"No, he was at work. It started to rain when we got there, and the boys helped bring their things inside. They were really happy to see their grandmother, and she was so very thankful for us. She thanked me over and over again for taking care of them, crying and hugging me. Boomie, they're in a good place, as their grandmother really cares for them," my wife said, her Australian accent growing thicker as the emotions surged within her. "When she started crying, I started crying, too. Of course, when I said goodbye to the boys, I cried even more. Even though they were excited to be home, they all cried when they said goodbye to me. I think it was nice for the grandmother to see that the boys were upset to leave. I mean," my wife continued, struggling with the words through her own tears that began to roll down, "she was able to see, I think, that the boys had been cared for, and that they were with a family that loved them. It was really very special, and I was glad that I could see it."

I was glad, too, to hear of this. So many times, we had seen the opposite, had seen children go back to environments that were not healthy, that were not positive. Indeed, there were times when some of the children did not want to leave our homes, like Sydney, and even Helena. Yet, I was still worried, worried that the boys would not receive the help and assistance they needed. Would we hear from them again? I hoped so, but my past experiences had told me no.

Chapter 6

For roughly the past nine months, we had been running on overdrive. Seven children were, at times, a little difficult. Difficult? It had almost done us in. For some odd reason that I could not explain, zombies were popular with the public, and Kelly and I felt like one of these undead. We were shuffling around, from one place to the next, with a glazed look in our eyes. Seven children had worn us out and taken much of our energy. The three in diapers were difficult, with each of their own personal issues, through no fault of their own. Heck, it was just tough to get three children in diapers ready each morning before work, while getting our own four ready for school. The three boys posed a different test each morning, day time, and evening, a test I am not sure that Kelly and I passed.

"I'm not sure I want to do this any more," my wife told me. It was early Saturday morning, and we were waiting in the terminal in the Atlanta airport for our flight to Zurich, Switzerland. Sitting next to me, she sipped from the last of her Starbucks cappuccino. In the past few years, she had voiced this concern, this desire of hers. Fostering was difficult for her, as she grieved each child's departure. She also questioned if we were doing enough for the children, and she voiced this concern a second later. "I don't think we are doing a good job, Boomie. I think the children are better off in other homes.

Besides, I don't know if I want to go through the sadness of losing any more children. It's hard…"

"I know, Sweetheart. It is hard," I replied. "But I think we are doing a good job. We are offering these children a safe and stable home, a clean home, and a healthy diet. We provide for them help with school work and, more importantly, a family that cares for them."

"But, Matt's, Logan's, and Derrick's family loved them too," she countered.

"Yes, but they weren't able to take care of them, and the boys had to be placed somewhere, Kelly, and there aren't enough foster homes; someone has to take care of these children," I added. "How about we just take a break for a while? Let's just not foster for a while after we get back from our vacation. Let's just focus on our own children when we get home."

She had heard this before from me, and I could see the skepticism in her smile. "We do need to take a break. I know, I know, every time I say I don't want to foster, I agree to take another child in," she said, smiling. Indeed that had been the case on a few occasions. My wife's heart always went out to these children in need, despite her own reservations. "This time, though, I mean it, Boomie. I think I'm done."

"I understand," I said. "Let's just take a break for a while and see what happens." Squeezing hands in acknowledgment, we both turned our attention to the children, who were patiently waiting to board the plane. Kelly and I were quite excited about the trip. As foster parents, we were not able to leave our foster children with babysitters, neighbors, or even family members, no matter the age, unless the individual watching the children had been drug tested, undergone a police background check, and been thoroughly inspected and trained through the foster care system in our state. This was due to the fact that the foster children in our care were not ours legally, but were in the custody of the state, and had to be cared for by those who had been cleared as trained and safe. After all, the child welfare agency in our state, and in all states, must ensure that foster children are in safe hands at all times. As a result, Kelly and I had not had a "date" since the previous summer, when we traveled to Arizona for the weekend during the Up With People reunion. Indeed, the two of us had not had a moment alone together outside the confines of our own bedroom walls. We were looking forward to an opportunity to speak to each other, to spend time together, and to simply enjoy each other's company, albeit surrounded by our own children.

Before we left, I had called Helena the evening before, for two reasons. First, I wanted to let her know that we would be out of the country if she needed us, and to contact us via email if an emergency arose. Second, I simply wanted to see how she was doing in college, with her first year just finishing. Though she had struggled with some courses, she was doing well, and had passed all of her classes. Despite the terrible circumstances she had come from and her personal history of such tragedy, sadness, and rejection, she was determined to graduate from college. Her drive and determination were inspiring to me, and I doubted I would be able to be as successful as she was. To be sure, I would not have been surprised, in the least, if she had become like the thousands of other foster children who aged out of the system. The Romanian had suffered greatly in her short life, and could have easily given in. Statistics showed that only 2 percent of foster children who aged out of the system would graduate from college. Helena needed a college diploma, if not to find a successful job, but to also find a reason to escape the environment she was currently in. She had returned to her adoptive parents of six years after aging out, moving back into their home. Not only had this family once abused and rejected her, they also encouraged her not to go to college, but to find a job immediately after graduating from high school. To counter this, I continued to encourage her with her dream of college with letters and phone calls, and Kelly and I both encouraged her to visit our home whenever possible.

As we would be gone for three weeks, we had hired someone to house sit for us. Taking care of the mail, feeding various animals, keeping the swimming pool clean, and a four day per week schedule of watering plants were all on the agenda for the young man who had recently graduated from high school. As my garden beds were large and extensive, and I had put many years worth of time and effort into them, I did not want to see them suffer or die off while we were away during the hot summer months. Gardening had become to me a place of refuge, a place where I could relax, leaving the stresses of work and fostering behind. Often times, I would pray and seek God's wisdom while digging in the dirt, hearing God's voice to me while planting a flower, pruning a bush, or planting seeds. Many times, I would take foster children into the gardens to help me, as Derrick, Matt, and Logan had done several times. The three had found much pleasure in my four compost bins, uncovering the composted garden scraps in search of worms. Derrick had even helped with the planting of many vegetable seeds in the early spring, just a few months back. My love of gardening had even spilled over into a bi-weekly garden column I wrote for some central Georgia newspapers, a hobby that I had enjoyed for the past six years.

We had been fortunate to receive some buddy passes from a friend of the family who worked with an airline. Certainly, on a teacher's salary, it would have been quite difficult to fly six people half way around the world to Europe and back, as tickets to Switzerland were rather expensive. These buddy passes allowed us to only pay for the airplane tax; the only drawback being that we were not guaranteed seats on the plane. In essence, we were flying "standby," boarding only if there were any leftover seats unclaimed on the flight. As there was no guarantee, Kelly and I were a little apprehensive that there would not be enough seats available. Fortunately, our names were called, and we boarded the plane last. Kelly and the three older children were even given the luxury of first class, while Grace and I rode in the very back of the plane.

Arriving in Zurich ten hours later, we were already worn out. We were soon faced with one of the challenges of traveling overseas in an international marriage. Kelly is not an

American citizen, but a permanent resident, instead, as was my status as well when I lived in Australia. Citizenship as an American for Kelly would cause her to give up her citizenship to her home land, something that would be unthinkable for all involved. Thus, when we arrived into Switzerland and faced the passports and customs section, we both were separated for a short time, as we both had different passports. Kolby, Jace, and Brody are all dual citizens, as both of their birth parents are from two different countries, and this time were traveling on their Australian passports, while Grace and I were on American ones. Once all were through, we found our luggage, and headed off to find our way to our next destination, Connie's house.

Connie was a fellow Uppie who traveled with Kelly and me back in 1990. Strangely enough, her husband, Hans, was the friend of Kelly's old German flame, Christoph. During our year of traveling, Kelly had of course spurned my advances of romance, and instead had harbored an attraction to Christoph, and he to her. This mutual admiration did turn into romance for the two, though fortunately for me, it was not to last for too long after our performing and travels had come to an end. Hans had met Kelly during our year of travel through his brother, though he was not romantically linked to Connie at that time. In an ironic twist that could only come through the power of love, Connie from Switzerland and Hans from Germany, two Uppies from different casts with Christoph as the common denominator, were married and now living in Germany.

Taking the train from Switzerland to Germany, Kelly and I struggled to stay awake on the two-hour trip, as we both began to suffer from jet lag. Though the plane trip was a short one in our eyes, only ten hours compared to the average 30 plus we spent traveling to Australia and Kelly's mother's home, we were struggling to keep our eyelids open, fearing we might miss the stop. Our concerns were happily not realized, and we soon found ourselves in the train station, and shortly after that in Connie's home. Now, we simply awaited the seventh member of our traveling troupe, Tim from Arizona. Tim was another former Uppie, and one that Kelly and I enjoyed visiting with at the previous year's reunion. Flying in on a separate flight seven hours later, he also wanted to visit with his European friends. By the end of the day, the Traveling DeGarmos Plus One were together, laughing and playing before falling asleep from jet lag.

After a few days of visiting with Connie, Hans, and their family, we boarded another train, this time on a scenic trip through the Swiss Alps. The trip was a breathtaking one, as the train wound itself in and out of the Alps in gorgeous fashion. After a six-hour trip, we found ourselves in a town straight out of the world of cinema; one that was majestic in its beauty. With the Alps surrounding us on all sides, we trekked off to the backpackers' lodge, suitcases in tow for each child and adult. Tim, Kelly, and I were full of excitement, yet a little apprehensive that we might not recognize some of those we traveled with over 20 years back. I, in particular, was looking forward to seeing Harri from Finland and Fredi from Switzerland, the two whom I had roomed with the most during our year of performing. As all three of us shared the same allergies, we were often placed in the same host families. Walking to the lodge, I smiled, recalling how Fredi would repeatedly talk in his sleep. On those frequent occasions, I would regularly wake him, imploringly beseeching him by saying "Fredi! At least speak in English so I can understand what you are saying!" Harri, with his broken English, did little to help me in this. Though we had arrived a day early, we did meet with Therese, from Sweden, who also was there a day before the reunion was to officially kick off, and we enjoyed a pleasant dinner, the four Uppies chatting a mile away, catching up with each other, while our younger children simply watched from the end of the table in awe, surrounded by foreign food, foreign languages, and foreign cultures.

The following day saw us catch up with Tommy, who hailed from Sweden. After wandering around the picturesque town and eating lunch, the children, Kelly, I, and our fellow Uppies headed back to the lodge. The two Swedes, two Americans, and the lone Australian were anxious to get back to the backpackers' lodge, hoping that our fellow reunion attendees would be there. As we rounded the corner of the tiny Swiss road leading to the lodge, the sound of uproarious laughter, mingled with shouts in various languages, including English, filled our ears, bringing smiles to all of the adults. Quickening our pace, and encouraging the children to do the same, we soon met up with a group of 20-plus adults, all laughing, all smiling, and all embracing each other. Kelly and I, along with Tim, Therese, and Tommy, soon dove into the mix, and quickly joined them in peals of laughter and joy.

Our concerns of not being able to recognize the others were soon dashed. There was Tim talking with Peter from Ireland and Hanne from Norway, Alex from Denmark was chatting with Taija from Finland, Zeljko from the Ukraine was laughing with Kunu from Switzerland. I looked over to see Kelly's large smile as she embraced her old flame Christoph, while Therese and Tommy had found Skip, another American who was living in the Ukraine. With so much excitement and laughter spread through the picnic area near the lake, where all had gathered, I didn't know where to first begin. This hesitation only lasted a few seconds, though, as I heard a familiar laugh. Turning my head, I found my two old roommates, Harri and Fredi, who were also laughing with great gusto, and I soon joined in with them. Fortunately, our own children were able to fend for themselves, and had soon mixed in with the other children who had been dragged to this reunion of crazy people from across the globe. Several of our friends had brought their own children along with them, and our children were busy attempting to break the barriers of communication that separated them. Glancing over at them, I was relieved to see each of my own children smiling, with looks of bemusement along with pleasure painting their own faces.

By the time Kelly and I had made it back to our small room, complete with two bunk beds, it was well past three a.m. We both were filled with joy, having seen people that we had not for years. Kolby and Grace lay in a top bunk, while Jace was in the other top bunk, while Kelly and I both attempted to find sleep in the two bottom bunks, and Brody lay on the floor with a host of blankets and pillows. Sleep did not come easy, as Kelly and I whispered to each other our thoughts and observations of the evening. Finally, sleep did come to Kelly, and I tried to drift off myself. All thoughts of fostering and the difficult times we had spent through the years vanished immediately. Perhaps for the first time in eight years, I was able to leave behind the grief, the heartaches, and the frustrations that had accompanied the many foster children that we had come to love in our home.

The next few days that weekend saw both children and adults climb the Swiss Alps, as well as visit some scenic locations. During the evenings, the adults were reliving old times with pictures, and even singing some old performing songs, all the time with tremendous laughter filling the lodge. Kolby, Jace, and Brody all had made new friends themselves, despite the differences in language, as each child taught the others new words and phrases in their own native tongues. I smiled to myself, one evening, as I peeked into the kitchen, finding a large group of international children playing cards. It was wonderful to see my own children make friends with others from across the globe. International relations were rather important to Kelly and me; after all, we were living in an international marriage. Indeed, it was also heartwarming to see Therese form a loving and caring relationship with Grace, as our little four-year-old followed the Swede everywhere that weekend.

Sadly, the weekend came to an end. Though I tried with all my might, I was unable to stop time from passing, as I wanted to stay with the group for a much longer period of time, perhaps for the next dozen years or so of my life, if possible; but freezing time in place was not a force that I possessed. Soon, we did have to make our goodbyes through tear-stained eyes, with the hope that we would see some soon at our next reunion, back in Georgia the following summer. Catching the train early that Monday morning, we soon headed off to a town in Italy, alongside the beautiful Lake Come, where Kelly had found a home we could rent for the next five days. After our stay there, we headed off to France, and spent several days in an old church monastery, historic for the fact that Joan of Arc had found refuge there herself hundreds of years ago. The love of history in me found it fascinating, as did our trip to Paris, where I soaked up the history of the fabled city with excitement.

By the time the three weeks were up, we were all exhausted, yet in a good way. Our cups had been refilled, as Kelly and I had found the stress and weariness that had been such a part of our lives the past few years slip away. Though we were sad to leave Tim, and the beauty that was Europe, my wife and I boarded the plane with our children, with a sense of peace. The laughter that had spilled forth from us during our trip left us refreshed. Even more, we were both truly relaxed, perhaps for the first time in several years. That sense of relaxation was about to come to an end though.

Chapter 7

"**K**elly, you won't believe this!" I said to my wife. Just a few minutes prior, I was in the kitchen, getting a glass of water, when the phone rang. After a quick conversation that left me almost laughing in disbelief, I walked out of the house and headed to the pool where my wife and children were. We had only been home one day since returning from our vacation overseas, and the children and Kelly were relaxing, as well as attempting to get over the jet lag that gripped their bodies. While my wife and children found the pool relaxing, I had found relaxation in a different way, spending the past two hours in the garden, transplanting some flowers, cutting back some stray asparagus, and generally cleaning up from the neglect of the past three weeks.

"Don't tell me she called again?" Kelly asked me, incredulous. She was floating in a long yellow inflatable lounging raft, a book in one hand, and a cold drink in the other. Her pink hat covered her face from the sun. Brody and Grace were playing tag in the pool, while Jace and Kolby lay on towels, soaking up the rays of the sun. Though I dearly missed our friends in Europe, it was good to be home.

"Yup, she sure did," I said, opening the gate into the pool area. Butterflies danced in the air around the 12 butterfly bushes that surrounded one side of the pool, while hummingbirds flew at neck-jerking speeds around the four feeders on either side of the pool house. The four cats were lazily sleeping under the many flowers, finding some relief from the late June sun. In the distance, one of the roosters was crowing, intermingled with the sound of ducks quacking. "This time, she wants to know if we can take a baby in."

Before we left for our trip, we had made it relatively clear to Cathy, the case manager, that we wanted a break for a while from fostering. Though Kelly had voiced that she did not want to foster any more, I held out hope that she would change her mind after some time had passed; at the very least, after a few months had passed. Yet, we had been home roughly 32 hours, and we had received four calls from DFCS; four calls regarding seven different children in need. The first call was for two children, ages six and seven, who needed placement into a home. Kelly took this call and, after a brief discussion with me, she told the case manager that we had just gotten home, and that we needed some time. We were given that time in the form of an hour. The second call was a teenage girl, 17 years of age, with a child of her own. I answered this time and, without hesitation, told Cathy that we could not handle this case, as we were not equipped, I felt, to take in a teenager who already had her own child. It was Kelly's turn, again, taking the third call, this time with three children in need of placement, ages 11, seven, and six. The answer was the same; we had just gotten home, and needed a break, and were not ready for seven children in the house again. At this point, I was finding it a little comical. DFCS, though, was desperate, and a few hours later called again. By this time, it was approaching seven in the evening, and they needed a home desperately. While I appreciated DFCS tenacity and the need for foster homes, we had only just gotten back from half way around the world, and, after all, we were supposedly just starting that break we had so desired. It was going to be a wonderful summer, and I was looking forward to a little less responsibility.

Apparently, God gave us a break. The break, though I was not aware of it at the time, was our holiday in Europe. That was evidently all the break we were going to have. "What is it this time?" my wife asked, raising her head from the book she was reading, comfortably floating on the raft.

"Well, this time, it's a baby; she's eight months old. Mom's on drugs and doesn't have a place to stay, as she is homeless. Cathy says it will probably be a long-term placement. She also said that she's sorry she keeps calling, but that she's desperate. She said she would understand if we said no again." During the brief conversation with Cathy a few moments ago, I had asked the case manager a number of questions in an attempt at gathering as much information as possible in order to share with Kelly. Through the years, my wife and I had come up with our own set of questions that we would ask when the Call was made to our home. The information, along with a great deal of prayer, helped us in determining whether or not we would take in that particular child. Up until just a few hours ago, we had only said "No" twice during the past nine years based on the information we received.

Taking a deep breath before releasing it in a sigh, Kelly put her book down on her lap. "Well, what do you think?"

"What do I think?" I asked, smiling at her. My smile was half born from the lunacy of the situation, the other from the irony of it. "Well, I don't want to take in another baby, but they are desperate."

"I don't either," she said before pausing for a moment. "Let's pray about it, and then you call her back with our answer."

"Okay," I agreed. Brody and Grace completely ignored us, while Jace and Kolby were listening in from their vantage point along the poolside. "Heavenly Father, we come to You for wisdom and guidance about this child. You know of our desire to take some time off. We are tired, and would like a break. But Lord, we want to do Your will and want to serve You in all we do. Please give us some insight on what we should do with this baby, and if You would like us to care for her. In Your name, we pray. Amen." Taking a deep breath, I looked over again at Kelly, putting forth the question a second time. "Well, what do you think?"

"I think you should call Cathy back and tell her we'll take the baby. What do you think?"

Though she had said that she was done fostering, I was not surprised by my wife's decision. Whenever a call had come in, and there was a desperate need to take care of a child who was suffering, Kelly's heart would always overpower us previous feelings on the subject. "Well, I think you're right. So much for our break," I replied, a nervous laugh escaping me. Immediately, my mind kicked into foster gear, and I began calculating all that needed to be done before the baby should arrive. We would need clothes, diapers, baby bottles, baby wipes, and I would have to get the baby crib out of the church attic, where our foster parent association was permitted to store any and all foster children items that were not being used. Before I did this, though, I needed to call Cathy back. A quick call to the caseworker to tell her that we would take the child was placed, and I was off to town to buy all that we needed, as well as to pick up the crib. Cathy was not sure when the child would arrive, other than to say it might be later on in the evening. As I drove off, Kelly and the four children went inside and began preparing for the arrival of the baby girl.

My mind was racing back and forth as I was walking down the diaper aisle. I could feel my anxiety level rise a little at the thought of changing diapers yet again. I had become quite the diaper expert the past 13 years, and could even change diapers with both eyes closed, and with no hands, or so it felt. Commander Diaper of the Diaper Patrol, the Don of Diapers, a Diaper Dynamo; all names that suited my position as Chief Changer of Dirty Diapers. Even though my status as the expert diaper changer in all of Monticello was one that was firmly in place, I did not look forward to yet another lengthy period of time changing baby diapers. Perhaps it was time for me to change my Facebook status under hobbies as "diaper changer" instead of "gardening."

It was ten o'clock that evening when we received a phone call from Cathy. According to her, the mother and child were nowhere to be found, as the mother had discovered that her child was to be placed into custody with foster care. As a result, the mother had run off with the child and was in hiding. DFCS and the police were looking for her, and Cathy informed us that she would get back to us in the morning with any updates. Breathing a slight sigh of relief that our night's sleep was to be an uninterrupted one, we both fell into bed, still exhausted from the jet lag.

It was early the next morning when Kelly took the Call, the fifth from Cathy in the past 24 hours. As I was up early, the time difference from one country to another still affecting my sleep patterns, I was in the garden at the time of the call. I could hear my bride call out to me from the back of the house, as our porch wrapped completely around the home on all four sides, an Australian style that Kelly incorporated into our new home when we built it.

"Morning, my love; what's wrong?" I greeted her, wiping away the early morning sweat atop my forehead. I had been hard at work digging a new flower bed, and the early morning humidity had already set in.

"Good morning. Well, I just got off the phone with Cathy, and the baby's not coming." Drinking from a cappuccino she had just made, my wife smiled at me with a grin that spoke volumes. I had been married to her long enough to tell that something was up, something was amiss.

"Why not?" I asked, waiting for some sort of announcement that I knew was coming.

"Well, they can't seem to find the mother. When I told Cathy that it was okay, that we were not too disappointed, she said, 'But…but…but…we have another baby girl for you.' I laughed, and told her that you had already gone out last night and bought a bunch of pink clothes for the other baby, so why not. What do you think?" she asked, smiling.

"Well, what do you know about the case?"

"The baby is 18 months old, and the mother is from here, in town. So is the dad, I think. They're not married, and there are drugs involved, I think on both sides. Cathy doesn't know how long the baby will be with us; it could be a while. Funny thing, though, the baby has been living with another family, though I really don't know too much on that. So, should we take her?"

"Sure, why not," I said. I had already given in to the fact that we were taking in a baby girl last evening, so the idea of one a few months older than we first planned upon didn't really matter too much. So much for that break we were hoping for. "Did Cathy say when the baby is coming?"

"Some time later this afternoon, after the other family she is living with gets home from work. I haven't told our own kids yet; they're all still sleeping. Since I'm up, I'll go and set the crib up in our room, and then I have to go to work for a few hours." Even though we had been home just a short time, Kelly dove right back into her massages, as her clients were excited to see her after the three-week vacation. Her job was an important one for us, as we depended upon the income it generated for our family. I was finishing up my own doctoral dissertation, and hoped to have it done by the end of the year. Our two incomes were necessary if we wanted to continue traveling back and forth between Australia and the USA. Though it was extremely expensive, especially with six in the family now, it was one of the challenges of an international marriage; someone was always going to be a long way from their homeland and family. Flying back and forth between the countries was no weekend trip. In fact, it took a weekend just to get to the other country.

It was just past seven that evening when the caseworker Anne sat down with Kelly and I to fill out the paperwork for the 18-month-old that had come to live with us. As usual, there were a great deal of papers to sign for Kelly and me. The lightly brown-skinned infant sat in Kelly's lap, a sad and forlorn lost look upon her face. "Myeisha was living with a lady by the name of Sue the past few weeks," Anne told us. "Apparently, the mother gave Myeisha over to Sue one day. She had met Sue in the grocery store a few times, and Sue had, I guess, shown some interest in Myeisha."

"You mean to tell me that the mother just gave away her child to a stranger?" I asked. While I had seen many things in my years as a foster parent, this was a new one to me.

"That's right," Anne answered. She had been a caseworker for a number of years, and had worked with us when we had Matt, Logan, and Derrick. I felt as if she found my questions tiresome and unnecessary, as her responses to me were not always pleasant ones. Kelly gave me a look that told me not to make her my new best friend with the jokes I usually rattle off with DFCS workers.

"So, how did DFCS get involved? How did this precious little one come into custody then?" This time, it was Kelly's turn to ask, as she hugged the tiny girl close to her chest.

Taking a drink from her cup of water and then moving the hair from her face, Anne looked tired, herself. As she was the only caseworker currently serving not only our own county, but three other counties in the area as well, she was overworked, overwhelmed, and underpaid. It was late in the evening, and she was anxious to go home herself. "Well, Sue was working full time, and was unable to take care of the baby. She called us to let us know that her work schedule was not allowing her to properly look after Myeisha."

"Well, it is obvious that this baby has been cared for," my wife said, "as she is the cleanest-looking foster child that has come to our home. Her hair is combed, her clothes are washed, and she looks healthy." Kelly was right; many of the children who had come to our home came covered in filth and dirt, with clothes reeking of smoke and other not so nose-friendly smells. This 18-month-old did come looking wonderful; hair was combed, clothes were clean, and she appeared healthy, to all indications.

"She does have some health concerns you need to be aware of," Anne said. "Sue says that she is allergic to red food coloring dye, so she isn't allowed to eat strawberries, raspberries, or anything that is red."

Perhaps Anne was simply tired and didn't realize the ridiculousness of her statement, but my wife sure did. As a doctor of naturopathic medicines and nutrition, people's eating habits were a primary concern of hers. "She can't eat strawberries because she's allergic to red food coloring?" she asked, in disbelief.

"That's right. Also, Myeisha doesn't go to sleep at night unless the television is playing. Sue had her fall asleep to the TV each night." I glanced over at Kelly, who also shared my amusement. Our own children were limited to an hour of the lone TV in our home each day. I saw little chance of this baby falling asleep to the sounds of television at night. Anne's suggestion reminded me of when Sydney's own mother demanded that we place a TV and DVD player in her daughter's bedroom, a demand that we were not able to meet.

"Does she have any siblings?" I enquired.

"Not on her mother's side, but she does on her father's," Anne replied, with an odd look on her face. "Her father has other children from other women. In fact, what is kind of strange is…" Anne stopped for a moment, head bowed, a peculiar smile hinted at around the corners of her lips. After a brief pause, she looked back up and continued. "What is unusual is that her father has a child with the mother's sister."

"The mother's sister?" This was most odd. I had heard of keeping it in the family, but this was way beyond that. Those most be some wild family reunions, I thought.

"Yes, that's right; her sister," Anne confirmed.

Trying to put that strange family relationship behind me for a moment, I went on. "Anne, I noticed that Myeisha's name is spelled differently on this paper," I said, indicating another form that we had to sign. On this document, the child's name was spelled "Myishea." Looking through the rest of the documents, I found her name spelled a third way, this time it was "Myeshia". This was not the first time we had encountered this problem. "Which one shall we use?" I asked.

"The first one, 'Myeisha,'" the caseworker said.

"Hi, Gracie. Why don't you take Myeisha and go play on the porch?" my wife suggested. By this time, Grace had wandered downstairs and had come face to face with a little girl her own skin color. While this had been the case with Linda, Micah, and Joshua, they were all too young to play with her, and Grace did not pay too much attention to the three. I was curious to watch my adopted daughter's reaction, remembering her comment eight months ago when she discovered that she was "brown." When asked what color I was, she replied, "Silly Daddy, you're yellow." I hoped that this would not be any kind of issue, as Kelly and I had stressed to our children over and over that we were all the same color, just different shades of God's skin. In this case, Grace showed no reaction, as our whole family was color blind in this area.

Finishing up the necessary paperwork with Anne, we bid her goodnight, and Kelly and I focused our attention on the newest member of the family. By this time, it was well past eight in the evening, and we needed to begin getting Grace to bed as well.

Since the time she first arrived an hour and a half earlier, Myeisha had not shown much emotion in her tiny frame. As is often the case, the child was afraid. She was surrounded by strangers in a strange home, torn suddenly away from all that was familiar to her. At 18 months of age, it was impossible for her to comprehend what was happening. Kelly's compassion for the small foster child soon overwhelmed her, and her mothering instincts quickly took over. After bathing the baby, Kelly attempted to feed her, but to no avail. The child's diet had consisted of junk food for so long that she was not used to the healthy and nutritious diet that was presented to her. I understood, myself, as it took me years to give up my diet of Fruity Pebbles, chocolate chip cookies, and ice cream and instead go on a much healthier diet. Unfortunately, my will power was much too weak, and I found myself on more than one occasion taking refuge in a closet, hiding from children, and giving in to my sweet tooth. Most days, the terrible trio that made up the Sweet Tooth attack was victorious, as my expanding waistline would testify.

After her attempts at feeding the young toddler had failed, Kelly placed Myeisha to bed inside the crib located in our room. Unlike the screaming Crack and Meth babies born addicted at birth, or the older ones who cried themselves to sleep, Myeisha simply lay there, staring up at Kelly, while a single tear dwelled in her left eye. The small child's unwavering gaze at my wife was full of profound sadness and heartbreaking rejection, and quickly moved Kelly to deep tears herself. I found her on the edge of the bed, next to Myeisha's crib, silently sobbing to herself, the grief of the child's own sorrow engulfing her. Kelly's many years as a foster parent had not prepared her for Myeisha's reaction, one the foster mother had not experienced before.

"Oh, Boomie, it's so sad," she said as I entered the bedroom. She valiantly tried to compose herself as she wiped the warm tears from her red face, but it was evident that she was deeply troubled. "I know she has been taken care of with Sue, but she's so very sad. She doesn't want to be here. Are we doing the right thing?" she asked poignantly.

"Sweetheart, we absolutely are doing the right thing," I tried to reassure her in as calm a voice as I could muster. I, too, was moved by Myeisha's plight, and found myself holding back the tears too. With the death of our own first daughter, Bronte, years ago from Anencephaly, a condition where the brain fails to grow, I had become very emotional, finding myself crying over any sad occasion. Children suffering in particular brought about strong feelings of sadness within me, and this one was no different. Refusing to give in to the emotions that swelled within my own heart, I attempted to comfort Kelly. "She was given away from her birth mother to a stranger, and this person couldn't take care of her. I understand that Sue took great care of her, and probably loved her deeply; but this baby was placed in DFCS custody, and therefore needed a place to go, my love." Placing my arms around her, I kissed her softly on the forehead, and felt her own body relax, the stress and tension retreating somewhat.

After she gathered her composure, a deep sigh broke forth from her before she responded. "I know, you're right," she said, and then moved over to Myeisha's crib. "Myeisha, I know you're scared, and I know you're lonely," my wife whispered tenderly to the newest child in our home, "but you are safe here, and we will love you and take care of you, okay? Now, I need you to go to sleep, and get a good night's sleep; everything's going to be all right." Bending down to kiss her on the cheek, Kelly covered the 18-month-old with one of the old blankets that had been used for countless other foster children in our home.

Taking my wife's cue, I also kissed the baby on the cheek, and caringly said, "Goodnight Myeisha, Jesus loves you." Taking Kelly's hand, we headed out to the kitchen and to our own children. The older ones had many questions, while Grace simply sat on my lap, taking it all in. Both Kolby and Jace were excited to have another small toddler in the house, and Grace liked the idea of someone closer to her own age. Left out yet again was Brody, who was not too delighted by the aspect of once again being the lone boy in a house full of girls. As we were all still suffering from the jet lag of our trip home, Kelly and I sent the four children off to bed, before attempting to find sleep ourselves.

It wasn't until midway through the next day that we were introduced to Myeisha's other side of her personality, a personality that was not pleasant, but instead rather disturbing. The quiet little 18-month-old we brought into our house was replaced by a much different child. In fact, the quiet aspect of her, the one that broke both Kelly's and my hearts, was exchanged with a loud and rather vocal one instead. We came to discover that Myeisha could speak, but her vocabulary was limited to two words, two words that Kelly and I had forbidden in our own home: "shut up."

"Shud up!" she said to Brody, as he passed her by. Kelly, Brody, Grace, Myeisha, and I were gathered together on the covered front porch, enjoying the warm weather, yet escaping from the heat of the noon-day sun at the same time. Kolby and Jace were still in bed, recovering from the long trip back from Europe.

"Myeisha, we don't say that in our house," Kelly told her, while Brody simply grinned from the rocking chair next to her.

"It's okay, Mom, I don't mind," Brody said.

"No, it's not, son. We don't want her to think that it's okay," she responded.

"Shud up!" our newest household member said again. Her inability to properly pronounce the word "shut" was cute, and brought a slim smile to my lips. Nevertheless, we weren't about to have Myeisha continue with it. Yet, before either Kelly or I were able to say something, she focused her attention on the cat that happened to walk by her. Without hesitation, Myeisha lashed out at the cat, hitting one of the calico felines that kept our yard mouse free. "Shud up!" she said, as the cat scrambled under the porch, unsure why it was the brunt of so sudden an assault from a human who was not much bigger in size.

"Myeisha!" Kelly said, raising her voice a little, with the tone of full parental mode coming forth in her thick Australian accent. "We do not hit cats, and we don't say 'shut up' either. We need to be sweet, okay?"

If Kelly expected Myeisha to respond in agreement, she was quickly disappointed. Instead, the foster toddler surprised all of us by throwing herself on the ground, screaming out in a childish tantrum, her legs and arms thrashing about in a fit. It was indeed a spectacle that neither of us were used to, nor were Brody and Grace, for that matter. Kelly and I did not tolerate temper tantrums in our household, and it had been a long time since we had seen one in action. Myeisha was in full force tantrum mode, with a high-pitched scream bellowing out of her tiny lungs that soon had the dogs in the neighborhood yelping in response.

Getting up from her rocking chair, Kelly calmly stepped over Myeisha, and in a most unruffled manner, serenely said to her, "Myeisha, we don't do this in our house. If you think I am not going to love you, you are already mistaken. You are going to be loved and loved and loved in our house, and nothing is going to stop us from loving you. So, get used to it," my wife said, with a smile spread wide across her face. She was right; we were fully prepared to love her unconditionally. This was a little child that had obviously been raised in a home where negativity and perhaps even violence reigned. That might explain the little one's lashing out to the cat and to each of us the next few weeks of summer. Yet, Kelly and I continued to speak soft and calming words to the 18-month-old, all the while loving her. Though we initially wanted to be on the break from fostering we so desperately yearned for, we realized that our path led elsewhere. Thus, the rest of the summer was spent showering Myeisha with as much love as we had for our own children. Yet, how long would the little one stay with us? The answer was one I never expected, nor even imagined.

Chapter 8

The summer had come to an end, and with it came a new school year. Kolby was now a high school student, beginning her freshman year at the high school where I worked. Brody was also at a new school, as he was now a sixth grader at the middle school. The new school year also saw me at a new school, too, as I began splitting my time between both the high school and the middle school. As a result, I was able to keep an eye on both Kolby and Brody, as well as Jace, who was now a seventh grader. Grace still had one more year until she began her school career in kindergarten, though she was anxious to begin now. Instead, like the three older ones before her, she continued to attend the local Baptist Church's Mother's Morning Out program, a service the church provided by looking after young children three hours a day. By this time, Myeisha was attending day care each day, the same center where many of our precious smaller foster children had also been enrolled. It seemed as if life were back to normal for us; school, work, and a house full of children.

Part of this normalcy for our family, though, was that there was little of it: normalcy. This was the case when we had agreed to provide respite for Tammy and Jason, two friends of ours who we had met years back when Kelly and I first met them during foster parent training. During those six months of training, my wife and I had become quite fond of the couple.

I particularly liked Jason as he would never cease to laugh at my jokes, thus encouraging me more each two-hour evening training session, despite the looks, pleas, and tight squeezes on my legs by Kelly to stop. Jason and Tammy were fellow foster parents in our town, and had adopted three girls of their own that had come through their home as foster children. For the past few months, they had been foster parents to two little boys, ages four and five. Though I had only met the boys once, at a foster parent association meeting, I had heard stories from both foster parents that they were a handful, and two tiny terrors.

It was mid September when we received a call from Tammy, asking if we could provide respite for the two boys. They were in the midst of moving from one home to another one, across town. Their problem lay in the fact that the new house was not yet ready to move into, and, as a result, they would be living in a rented home for roughly a month's stay, as they awaited the opportunity to move into their new home. As one of the policies of DFCS stated that foster children needed to be in a home owned by foster parents, the boys would not be permitted to accompany Tammy, Jason, and their three daughters during their brief sojourn in the rented house. Kelly and I happily agreed to help by taking the two boys in for the month. After all, we had discovered that there wasn't much difference between five children and seven children, with the main exception being that we would once again need two cars to transport our large family back and forth.

Tammy and Jason's house displacement reminded me of our own nearly ten years ago. Kelly and I had decided to sell our own home and build another one on a larger piece of land. A month before our new home was finished, the one we were living in sold, and we moved out. Our main dilemma, though, lay in the challenge of finding a place to rent for a month. After a few places did not work out, we moved into the basement of our own unfinished home, minus electricity and plumbing. The builders rushed to finish the house on the ground and top floors, placing in hardwood floors, painting, and other tasks that go along when a house is being built. At this stage, our oldest, Kolby, was four years old, Jace three, and Brody a year and a half.

Those late October evenings saw darkness descend upon us around six p.m. and, with it, bedtime as well for our young family, as there was no electricity to see by. No lights meant no visibility. As all the furniture and belongings we owned surrounded us in our unfinished basement, Kelly and I simply placed the mattresses that were leaning against the walls in the day time onto the floor and tucked each child into bed by the glow of candlelight. It was during these evenings that we would fall asleep listening to the sounds of mice scurrying across the floor around us. Indeed, one time we found a snake in the basement with us. As there was no plumbing, toiletry issues posed a problem, and a plastic bag lining a bucket usually was the solution. For those more dire emergencies, a trip to the local grocery store offered relief. Showering often occurred at a church friend's house. It was either a month of great discomfort or one of character building; I chose to think of it as the latter, though it was a month that Kelly wished never to revisit.

Jason dropped the boys off at our house on Sunday afternoon after church. Five-year-old Steven and four-year-old Jack certainly looked harmless enough upon first glance. As Jason and I brought their clothes and the other few belongings they had into our house, the two boys ran around outside like two normal boys their age. Kelly met us at the door with Myeisha in her arms, as usual, as our own small foster child enjoyed the comfort and security found in my wife's embrace. Racing in behind us, Steven and Jack tore past us and attempted to enter the kitchen before Jason was able to stop them. Bending down and looking in each face, he reminded them that they were to be on their best behavior in our home before telling each that he loved them. The boys echoed back their love to him, giving him a hug, and then turned their attention to Kelly, who offered them her customary chocolate cookies, holding one in each of her hands. The boys happily accepted, and began devouring their treat while Kelly looked on. Jason then asked me to walk out on the porch with him to fill me in on the boys.

"They were living with their grandfather when DFCS took custody of them," the father of three told me. "The grandfather was abusive to them, and cursed at them all the time. DFCS got involved when they found out that the grandfather tried to sell the boys for five hundred dollars."

"You're kidding!" I exclaimed, horrified and saddened at the same time. "Oh, the poor boys. They must be a mess," I said, thinking of their emotional state. Abused, cursed at, and objects to be sold; the thought of it troubled me greatly.

"Oh, they're a mess, all right," Jason said with a tone of warning in his voice. "They are wild, John. They're the most wild we've had in our house. They curse all the time, and run around constantly. If Jack doesn't take his medicine, he's even worse. Believe me, John, they're exhausting."

How wild could they be, I thought to myself. Surely they can't be too bad. Besides, they looked cute and harmless enough. My friend Jason must have been merely exaggerating. "Not to worry, Jason, they'll be just fine."

"It's not them I'm worried about," he answered back with a laugh. "Believe me, John, you've got your hands full with them. They will…"

"Ahhhh…" Jason was cut off by Kelly, who staggered out the front porch door, looking completely and 100 percent flabbergasted. In my 20-plus years knowing the Australian, I had never seen her speechless like she was before us. "Ahhhh…" she repeated, this time with a mixture of half smile, half befuddlement.

"What's wrong?" I asked her, curious as to what could leave her in such a state.

"The boys…you won't believe what one of them just said." Her voice trailed off, instead replaced with nervous laughter, bewilderment painting her lovely face.

"What?" I simply asked, as Jason watched the two of us as an interested spectator. I suspected he wasn't surprised by the confusion that my wife was internally battling.

Taking a long pause to compose herself, Kelly looked at the two of us, eyes wide open. "Well, I was talking to the boys, asking them a little about their teachers at school, when Gracie started coming down the stairs. She was upstairs with Kolby and Jace. When she started coming down, one of the boys, Steven I think, looked at her and said…and said…" Her accent thickened with emotion. She then looked at me with wrinkled brow and creased forehead, and presented a most odd and peculiar smile; one that bespoke of astonishment and great surprise.

"Said what?" I enquired.

"He said…he said," Kelly paused, trying to gather herself. With an effort, she finally was able to relay the story to us. "He said, 'Look at the little nigger girl. Hey, little nigger girl, come here!'"

"*What?*" I exploded, the shock registering across my own face.

"He called Gracie the 'n-word,'" Kelly said in a half whisper. "I don't think he knew what he was saying. He was smiling, and wanted to play with Grace. Fortunately, she doesn't know what the word means."

"I told you so," said Jason, with a slight smile upon his lips as he stood as an observer throughout this. "Those boys are rough."

"What did you do?" I asked.

With her mouth agape, a laugh of incredulity came forth from her before she began to reply. "Nothing! I didn't know what to do. I just stood there, thinking 'He didn't just say that, did he?' I was in shock!" Rarely had I seen my wife in such a state, as she is usually very quick on her feet. Holding the door open for both her and Jason, I suggested we go back inside and start damage control. What I heard next propelled me to race hastily across the room.

"C'mon, Stevie, let's pee in da cornuh, and not da toilet," the four-year-old said, facing the corner of the kitchen. He had begun pulling his pants down, as his older brother walked toward him, anxious to join in with the festivities. Apparently, these two had immediately felt right at home, and had made our house their personal lavatory.

"Yeah, dat's cool!" his brother responded, with equal enthusiasm.

"No, no, no, no, no!" My words fired out of me at a machine gun staccato pace. Frantic to hinder their adventure in urine in my kitchen corner, I propelled myself forward, scooping up Jack in one arm, and his brother in the other, before taking them outside on the porch. Looking at each of them with vexation, I attempted to make it quite clear to the boys that their decision to use my kitchen as an indoor outhouse was not a wise or valid one. "Boys, we do *not* go to the bathroom in the kitchen. That is a very big no-no, okay?"

"Okay," the two replied in unison, smiles across both faces.

"Boys, let's go say goodbye to Mr. Jason one last time," I said, taking each by the hand and leading them back outside to Jason's car. We bid him goodbye and then went back into the house. The rest of the evening was spent chasing after the boys from one room to another and trying to curb their constant cursing. Kolby, Jace, and Brody often shot Kelly and I looks of shock and awe, as the two boys spewed forth profanity as if it were an everyday thing for them. Sadly, in the environment the two boys grew up in, it probably was their norm.

After watching the clock for well over four hours, the small hand finally crept to seven, and it was bedtime for the boys. Indeed, Kelly and I were relieved that bedtime had come; the boys had worn us out in such a short time. As we had moved the bunk beds that Matt, Logan, and Derrick had slept in long ago to a storage facility at our church and had instead finally turned the room into the guest room that Kelly had wanted for so long, the room now only sported a queen-sized bed in an antique white iron bed frame. Though we were both tired, we read the boys a story, said a short prayer with them, and kissed each on the forehead before turning off the light, leaving the night light in the room on. Any hope, though, that we would find relaxation during the evening hours was foolish, as both Kelly and I spent the remainder of the evening taking turns going back and forth to the boys' room. Steven and Jack apparently felt no desire to sleep, as it seemed that they found our queen-sized bed a trampoline designed to be used while wearing pajamas. Each time Kelly or I made our way to their room, they were jumping on the bed. This lasted for the next three hours, and only ceased when they began arguing between each other, lasting another hour. Another sleepless evening as foster parents, though this time it was not because of crying; this time it was simply boys being boys, albeit rather wild.

In fact, they were wild not only that night, but for the next day, the day after that, and again after that. Truth be told, they were by far the wildest bunch of human beings that Kelly and I had ever encountered. Full on wild! Wild at heart! Boys gone wild! These two boys were Mack trucks running on full speed leaving a path of destruction in their wake like I had never seen before. By the second day, Tuesday, our house was almost unrecognizable, a pig sty and a garbage pit. There were toys strewn from one end of the house to another, and dirty clothes littered not only the floor of their own room, but through many rooms. Kelly and I were having a hard time keeping up with the two, and were failing miserably at that. Their behavior while at their day care was not any better, as both boys were in trouble daily for excessive talking, getting out of the seats constantly, and for profanity in the classroom. Though they were extremely cute and good natured, they reminded me of two feral dogs, completely wild. As wild and as uncontrollable as they were, Kelly and I found ourselves laughing through it, as we didn't know quite how to respond to their actions, their deeds, and most especially to their words. Kids say the darnedest things, with these two living proof. Since the boys were only staying with us for a short time, one month, we decided to basically roll with the many punches the boys were throwing. Perhaps we were simply punch drunk from their zest, their gusto, and their pastime of annihilation, demolition, and obliteration.

Perhaps God was having mercy on us when Tammy called Kelly Thursday evening, telling us that they would pick up the boys after school the following day. What was initially supposed to be a month ended up being just five nights, as they were able to find a place to live; one that DFCS approved of. Those five nights seemed as if they were closer to five months, and it was with little disappointment that I said goodbye to the boys. Though I very much enjoyed helping Tammy and Jason out, I also felt that our house needed to be spared from any more substantial collateral damage.

Myeisha was adjusting well to our home and to our family. As I suspected, she made a big impact at our church. Her cute smile had woven its way into several of our church members' hearts, and there were many Sunday mornings where Kelly and I were met at the church door by people who wanted to hold her. Once again, we were blessed with such a loving and supportive church family; we truly would not be able to serve as foster parents if not for their help.

We had been able to rid Myeisha of her special phrase, "shut up," though it did take some time and patience from our end to accomplish this, and was no easy task. What we found instead was that her vocabulary was severely limited beyond that, and the few words she could say were said in a very poor fashion, making it quite difficult to understand her. Her speech patterns were far below others her age, and required a great deal of attention from Kelly and myself. Her demeanor had changed, as well, with both the passage of time, and the loving attention that Kelly and I showered upon her. We had come to the belief that by completely surrounding her in positive attention, love, and compassion, her harshness, negativity, and violent outbursts would subside. Fortunately, this approach did work, leaving us with an incredibly sweet-natured child. Instead of lashing out to others and hitting anything walking past her, Myeisha now would run to hug Kelly, I, or any of the children when one of us would return from outside the home. Indeed, the little one enjoyed being held, and craved the attention of others.

Looking back at those first few months with her, I shuddered thinking about the environment she must have initially grown up in during her young life; an environment that had taught one so very young to hit others and to yell "shut up!" to anything within her range of vision. In truth, this thought did more than make me shudder; it angered me. I was disturbed that those who were to protect this tiny child, to raise her in a loving home, and to provide a positive example for her had instead subjected her to an environment of violence and negativity. Like Steve and Jack, no child should be in an environment that was so hateful and so negative. Indeed, young children should also not have such disturbing words in their own vocabulary. Jack and Steve had learned their words of hatred from their grandfather, while Myeisha had learned hers from those who were raising her. Yet, my own anger at this was a reflection of my own personal judgment upon these others; judgment that I knew was wrong. After all, Jesus had clearly warned countless times about the dangers of judging others. Matthew 7:5 was also clear by stating "You hypocrite, first take the log out of your own eye, and they you will see clearly to take the speck out of your brother's eye." I was very much a sinner, had wronged many others on a daily basis with my own selfishness, pride, and judgment; who was I to judge the actions of others? This was something I very much needed to spend time on in prayer, as I was having a difficult time loving my fellow man, no matter how much they had hurt these children. Jesus said to love one another; why was I having a hard time loving these people?

* * *

Our tiny town of Monticello fully showed the seasonal changes that autumn brought with it. Trees were losing their leaves, and those leaves that still clung tenaciously to their branches were shades of orange, yellow, and brown. Pots filled with chrysanthemums adorned many homes, while rose bushes feebly presented the last blooms of the year. Swim suits and summer clothing were replaced with warm jackets and hats. Friday nights saw the town come out to the local football field in hopes that the high school would pull off a victory. As Kolby was a member of the high school's marching band, we joined the town in the autumn tradition. It was not nearly as rough as rugby, Kelly's homeland version of football, and I tried to explain to her the complex set of rules that accompanied the sport. I found, though, that the sport did not interest my Aussie wife at all, as she instead found much more enjoyment simply socializing with her fellow spectators. My wife had the ability to make people feel special, as her warmth and natural charm were always on display to all she met. With the addition of Myeisha to our brood of children, Friday night football games were an adventure each week. The little one turned heads, as people were always anxious to see the newest member of our household, and even more eager to hold her.

It was during the second home game of the season, though, that we found that life with Myeisha might pose some of the challenges that we also faced with Grace. Like Grace, Myeisha's biological mother and father were both from the small burg of Monticello. As the population of the entire county was well under 10,000 residents, with the town again much smaller than that, it seemed that everyone knew everyone else. This can be wonderful when raising children; a small-town atmosphere that offered security and family values. At the same time, it had also presented problems for Kelly and me, as we would often encounter people who stated that they were Grace's relatives. As we did not know who her biological father was, I had early on decided that she would not be able to date anybody in the six surrounding counties, as it could be a relative of hers.

On this particular evening, Kelly and I, along with Jace, Brody, Grace, and Myeisha, were standing in line, waiting to pay to enter into the football stadium. Dusk was settling into the early October sky, and there was a slight chill in the air. Kelly was carrying the baby bag, as well as a cushion for herself, while I had Myeisha in my right arm, and was holding Grace's hand with my own left. Without warning, I felt Myeisha lifted from my arm, without invitation, as a voice loudly assailed me. "Hey Meemee! How ya doin?" The stranger's voice squealed in a shrill tone. As the interruption was so very sudden, I was unprepared for the small child to be taken from me, and swung quickly around to see who had taken our young foster daughter from me. Since Kelly and I were legally responsible for Myeisha as her guardians, I was especially bothered by this. As I turned quickly to face who had taken her, I found Myeisha looking uncomfortable in the arms of a teenager, a young girl who was holding the squirming child. In fact, the teenager was a child herself, so very young. "Dis is Meemee!" she said, her high-pitched voice assaulting all within earshot of her. Surrounding the teenage girl were a number of other children, all her age.

Few times in my life am I speechless, and this was one of those times. Unfortunately, my experience with biological family members had not been pleasant ones in the past. I had been cursed at, spat upon, had objects thrown at me, while Kelly had even been followed while driving by a set of angry birth parents. As a result, I was quite wary any time I met someone who claimed they knew one of our foster children. This time, it was taken a step further, as the foster child was taken from me without permission. As a result, all I could blurt out was, "Ah…yes, this is Myeisha… She is living with us right now."

"Hey Meemee! 'Member me?" The teenage girl held Myeisha in front of her, arms extended, while the 21-month-old child looked back at me. Was that a look of fear upon her face? I could not tell, but it was clear that she was not at ease. Without hesitation, I gently placed my hands around Myeisha's mid section, and with as much politeness as I could muster, pulled her back towards me.

With her in my arms, safe, it was time for me to put on my Sherlock Holmes detective hat and find out who the stranger was that had plucked Myeisha from me so swiftly and brazenly. "Hello, I'm Mr. DeGarmo, and you are?"

"Hey, Mista Garma," the teen replied, her voice not wavering one bit in its volume. "Ah knows ya, yur da new liburian at my school."

"Ah, yes. How are you doing?" Through the growing darkness of the evening, I was able to recognize her as indeed one of the students at the middle school, though her name escaped me. Was this a relative of Myeisha's, I wondered. I didn't have to wonder very long, though, as the young child, probably only 10 or 11 years older than the one securely in my arms, now answered.

"A'm good," she said, her voice lowered a little, though still shrill in tone. Pointing to Myeisha, she continued. "That's muh Meemee. She usta live wit me and my mumma," she said, before placing her hand on the child's shoulder. "Hey Meemee, how ya doin?" she asked, the foster child clinging to me, anxiety filling her face. "Meemee, wat's da mattuh? Doncha remembah me?"

Trying to make all feel a little more comfortable in this awkward situation, I encouraged Myeisha to respond to the teenager who was so adamant in her relationship with the displaced foster child. "Say hello, Myeisha." For a response, the toddler only snuggled further into my jacket, shielding her face from the middle-school child. Looking for an avenue to escape from the crowd of friends supporting the teenager that was slowly gathering in force to surround us, I took a hold of Grace's hand, which I had let go of moments before when reclaiming Myeisha. "Okay, enjoy the football game. I have to catch up with the rest of my family. Bye," I said, forcing a smile to my lips as I rushed off to catch up with Kelly and the other children. She had been oblivious to the entire incident, as she had been eager to see Kolby and the marching band perform the pregame songs, and was thus a few paces ahead of us in line. Quickly, I shared the small tale of Myeisha's close encounter with her.

"That must have been Sue's daughter," she told me, with a look of concern on her face. "I don't like that the girl just grabbed Myeisha out of your arms. What if it were someone trying to take her?"

"I agree, Kel," I said, holding Myeisha a little closer at the same time. "That's just part of the problem of living in the same small town that our foster children have family in." Indeed, it was a problem, but one that I was prepared to face.

* * *

"Mr. DeGarmo, we need you to come pick up Myeisha from day care right now."

Susan's voice had a note of alarm in it that Thursday afternoon in early November. Susan worked at the day care where we had been taking many of our foster children throughout the years. Usually when she called, I would have to leave work and take a sick foster child home, and had done so several times in the past. As it was much more difficult for Kelly to cancel her appointments on such short notice, it was up to me to take time off of work, looking after sick children. This time, though, Susan's voice had a little more urgency in it.

"Is she sick?" I asked, sitting back in my chair at the high school.

"No, but there's been a little fire at the day care, John, and we need to have everyone pick up their children. Nothing serious, just the air conditioning unit is causing a lot of smoke."

"I'll be right there!" I said, and rushed out to let the front office know of the emergency. As the town of Monticello is so small, I arrived at the day care within moments, and whisked the child home. Fortunately, it was only a fan belt that had caught on fire, and was easily taken care of. This was the second time that week that Susan had reached me with some sort of concern. Both incidents were clearly not the fault of the day care, as they had been so very helpful to Kelly and me, eager to assist us in any way when we had foster children.

Apparently, Myeisha's birth mother had moved in next door to the day care and had been making unsupervised visits to see her daughter, talking to the small child over the fence on afternoons. As her child was in care of DFCS, the child welfare agency, all visitations between child and biological family members had to be supervised by either a caseworker, or one trained by DFCS. The unsupervised visits were bad enough; what compounded the problem was who accompanied her. The troubled young mother was bringing over some of her friends with her when she visited her daughter, friends that were of questionable integrity, friends who bespoke trouble in their actions and their reputations around the small town. Friends we were quite uneasy about. Visions of the small child being lifted up over the day care fence and taken away by strangers filled my head. She was in jeopardy; these unsupervised visits by her mother were putting Myeisha in danger, and had to cease immediately. As a result, I encouraged Susan to call the police immediately if the mother should arrive again unannounced. I also placed a call to the caseworker, Anne, to let her know of the situation, and the danger that the mother placed not only Myeisha in, but all those at the day care. After all, the mother's friends might place the day care at risk by sudden and unexpected actions. Anne reassured me that she would speak to the mother about it, and inform her that she was not allowed to continue with the unsupervised visits, and that she was in violation of the case plan she needed to complete in order to regain custody of her daughter.

It was becoming apparent early on in our fostering of Myeisha that we were going to have our hands full, in a variety of ways. I just prayed that God gave us the strength and the wisdom to meet these challenges, because I knew I wasn't equipped to do it on my own.

Chapter 9

Christmas was once again soon approaching, and with it came the excitement that the holiday brought. Brody and I had traveled to a local tree farm and brought home our traditional 11-foot tree the day after Thanksgiving. After setting it up, the family adorned it with a hodgepodge collection of Christmas tree decorations while dining on homemade cookies and hot chocolate. For Kelly and I, this was indeed our favorite holiday, as it brought so much joy in so many ways. The joy of Christ's birth, along with the joy of Santa Claus for the little ones, created a magical buzz in our home that was second to none.

As we had a house full, Kelly and I had a great deal of shopping to do, in order to help out Santa during this busy time. After all, I did not want to burden him with so many children in one stop. Kelly did the bulk of the shopping, as she enjoyed the opportunity to have some time to herself while I looked after the children. As it is for foster parents in our state, we were unable to both leave the children with a babysitter, so that meant no shopping together or no date night for the two of us. The children were in our custody, and DFCS did not permit us to leave the children in someone else's care, unless that person was properly trained by the child welfare agency, had undergone police background checks, house inspections, fingerprinting, and a host of other obstacles. This policy surely made it difficult for married couples, resulting in Kelly and me working hard to have any one-on-one conversation, as it seemed there were always children around. Oftentimes, these adult conversations were done in the only true sanctuary we could find; our closet, The Closet of Solitude, as I referred to it, as children seemed to be always walking into our bedroom every time we tried to have a moment's conversation. Thus, the closet became our new conversation hall. There, amongst clothes, shoes, jackets, hats, scarves, and the many mismatched socks, Kelly and I were able to discuss matters of importance that directly impacted our lives and the lives of the children in our home.

The past three years had seen me hard at work on my doctoral dissertation, and I was nearing completion. All that remained was for me to defend it before a committee at the university I was attending. Through the years as a foster parent, I had seen a number of children come through my home that struggled tremendously with school, both with academics and behavior. Not only did they struggle, but I had been witness to my fellow teachers struggling, too. Most teachers did not have the resources, skills, or training to help the foster children in their classrooms. More than this, like the general public, many teachers simply did not know much about how the foster care system worked, nor about the many challenges that foster children truly dealt with on a day-to-day basis. Those in education did not appreciate the fact that when a foster child is removed from a home and placed suddenly into a strange home with strangers, without warning, school was often the last place the child wanted to be. Instead of focusing on a new school, new teachers, homework, and all that comes with school, most foster children are filled with fear and simply wish to return home, as school was the least of their priorities. As a result, these children struggle mightily in school, as I had seen time and time again with my own foster children. With this in mind, I decided to devote my doctoral studies to not only the foster children who had come through my own home, but for foster children everywhere. My dissertation explored not only these challenges, but also presented many strategies designed to best aid foster parents, caseworkers, and teachers as they all worked to help foster children in schools.

As the university was located in another state quite some distance away, I was able to do much of the work online. My dissertation defense was also online and was the last step in a long and arduous process in obtaining my doctoral degree. I was eager to complete it, if only to look my wife in the eye as a fellow doctor. We had both decided to obtain these degrees as an attempt to show our own children, and our foster children, the importance of not only education, but that learning was a lifelong process for all.

Four days before Christmas saw the entire family home, all seven of us. It was the first day of Christmas vacation, and I was scheduled to have my defense of my dissertation at one that afternoon. Kelly had come home early from work at noon, permitting me to prepare for the meeting online with the members of the committee. I had prepared an exhaustive PowerPoint presentation on the paper, rehearsing it several times beforehand. My biggest worry, though, was the possibility of an invasion; an invasion of children interrupting the presentation. Therefore, I asked Kelly to ensure that all the children were quiet upstairs, as I would be in the library, in the basement, presenting the PowerPoint online. The door in the house leading to the basement was locked, as were the three doors outside leading into the house from the basement level. All four doors had large "do not disturb" signs taped on them. The last thing I wanted during the video conference was a crying baby, arguing children, or the thunder of feet through the house; all sounds that seemed to ring throughout our house on a constant basis.

The presentation went by quickly, as did the next hour, and by two o'clock, I had completed my last requirement for the program. Powering down the computer, I allowed myself a small bit of satisfaction before heading back upstairs and into the general clamor that resided in our home. Apparently, becoming a doctor didn't bring any peace or quiet to the household; Myeisha was already crying from the bedroom.

* * *

"Kel, I don't feel so well." For the past few hours, my stomach had been bothering me. It was just past noon on Christmas Eve, and Kelly was preparing her traditional large Christmas Eve meal. An air of excitement reigned in the air, as the children were anxious for the day to end and Christmas to arrive. For some odd reason, my wife enjoyed December 23rd, referring to it as "The Eve of the Eve of Christmas Day." To celebrate, we went out to dinner on the day, giving Kelly a break from the chore of cooking a large meal for a large family.

"What's the matter?" she asked me, placing my favorite, pumpkin pie, into the oven. Desserts, mashed potatoes, stuffing, freshly baked bread, and a leg of lamb, shipped from Australia, blanketed the kitchen counters, as Kolby and Jace helped the preparations for the big meal.

"My stomach hurts a bit," I said, holding onto my side. It had been around 24 hours since we ate at the restaurant. Since then, my stomach had grown increasingly weaker, as pain began to overwhelm it. "I hate to say it, Sweetheart, but I'm not so sure I can eat anything for dinner."

"Hmmm. I hope it's not food poisoning," she said, wiping her hands on a towel. "Brody and Grace have been complaining about the same thing."

I hoped not, either. Not only did I not want to miss out on the pumpkin pie, as well as the rest of the food, but I was also singing a solo at church later on in the evening. Yet, food sickness it was, for all three of us, as Grace, Brody, and I spent the rest of the afternoon and evening sick to our stomachs. My wife called the church to inform them of my plight, and inability to perform that evening, while I weakly looked on from the coach in the lounge room. Grace and Brody lay in the adjoining couches in the room as well. Kelly's role as chef was quickly changed to house nurse, as she tried to not only minister to our health woes, but cleaned up after Grace and Brody disposed of any food in their bodies in a very Grinch-like fashion. I felt as if all of the ghosts from Dickens's classic story *The Christmas Carol* were residing in my stomach, churning it into a tumult of ghastly woes. Not only did my stomach go out, but my heart did, as well, towards my wife, cleaning up vomit from the younger children, taking care of Myeisha, and getting no help from me in the process, all on Christmas Eve. In my condition, I was not much help to her later that evening, after all the children had gone to bed, as she prepared for Santa's arrival.

Fortunately, by midday on Christmas Day, the three of us were feeling better, and we were able to enjoy the day as a family. Once again, Lynne and Steve helped us out with gifts for Myeisha. The two dear friends had appointed themselves foster grandparents to any of our foster children, helping us out with gifts at Christmas time. Kelly and I were both filled with gratitude for both Lynne and Steve, and considered them a blessing from God. With their help, and with the help of others, we were able to ensure that Myeisha's Christmas was a special one. Our own children had come to understand that foster children in our home would receive more gifts at Christmas time than they would, as Kelly and I tried to make Christmas a very magical one for these children in need. We had found through the years that many foster children never received gifts at Christmas. Even sadder was that many of these same children had never had a birthday gift or even a card, let alone a birthday party. This fact greatly affected me; how could a child not have a birthday present on his special day? Birthdays were supposed to be special days for a child, a day that was to be celebrated in his honor. Indeed, every child should have someone sing "Happy Birthday" to him, and have at least one gift to open. Both Kelly and I decided early on in our fostering to make sure that birthdays, Christmas, and other holidays were to be special for foster children in our homes. I only hoped that it wasn't the only time these foster children were able to celebrate these special days after they left our home.

* * *

I put the children's book back on the shelf and walked downstairs to the kitchen while Myeisha and Grace followed behind me, waiting for me to prepare them a midday snack. The two little ones had been sitting next to me while I read them a book, and now were hungry. Kolby and Jace were doing some laundry, and Brody was playing a game he had gotten for Christmas. All throughout the day, I was unable to shake the dream I had the night before, as it refused to leave my mind. Earlier that morning, my slumber was interrupted by a disturbing dream, one that troubled me so much that I was unable to properly focus on anything else that I attended to. It was three days past Christmas, Kelly was back at work, and I was taking care of the many duties in the home, as well as the children. As always, the children were a handful and required much of my attention with Myeisha in particular. Yet, there was one child who was foremost on my mind: Sydney.

The dream that woke me around four that morning continued to replay itself in my mind. I had dreamt that Sydney was lost and was trying to find us. Our former foster child was alone and scared, wandering through a forest, looking for Kelly and me in the dream, and neither of us were able to come to her aid. The image of her calling out "Daddy, Daddy," over and over again, was deeply unsettling to me, as it weighed heavily on my heart. It had been six years that Christmas season since she left our home, and two years since she called our house, and her absence was keenly felt. Indeed, I continued to pray for her daily, hoping that she was in a place where she was loved and taken care of. Sadly, I suspected that she was not in either place, as the last we had heard, when we received that unexpected phone call a few years back, was that she had been placed into a group home. My experiences visiting Helena in a group home were not pleasant ones. To be sure, these group homes were places where foster children could go and live, a true blessing for those children who had no place to call home. Yet, I had found that with Helena's group home, it was not a very nurturing and loving environment. With this group home, there were ten foster children per home, with an adult assigned on a rotating schedule to look after the children. Like Helena, the other foster children in the home had been bounced from home to home, and many of them were either unable to function and live in a foster home, or were considered "unadoptable," the term I was presented with by the group home. As Sydney's last foster mother had told us that our former foster child fitted both groups, unadoptable and unable to function, I was certain that she was in a difficult place in her life. In other words, I imagined that she was a mess, and that we might, sadly, regret contacting her, as she would be so disruptive in our lives.

Even though Sydney might bring some chaos into our lives, I wanted to find her, to reach out to her. I wanted to let her know that she was loved, that she was thought of, that she was important, and that she mattered. The phone call I received two years back, after she had been away for many years, had never left my mind, and had never stopped bothering me. Sydney's voice, calling me "Daddy" in a plea of desperation, had deeply unsettled me. I had to find her; I had to locate her. This poor girl, part of our home for so long, was in need, the need to be loved and cared for. My chief concern was that Kelly and I might be the only family for this young girl, the only ones who might tell her that she mattered, that she was significant. We might be the only people who would tell her that we loved her, something that each child deserved to hear every single day.

I hated the thought that Sydney might end up like the thousands of other foster children in the United States each year that aged out of the system. These foster children, after usually reaching the age of 18, are no longer cared for by the state and by the child welfare agencies, nor by foster parents. As many of them drop out of school, they often face the world with no job skills and with poor social skills, as well. Far too many of them end up on the streets, homeless and unemployed. Along with this, the majority of these former foster children have emotional challenges they struggle with, mental health issues that are not treated, keeping them from success. Heavy drug use, high pregnancy rates, and even higher rates of criminal action all were end results for many foster children. Fortunately, Helena was driven to steer clear of this path, as she had aged out of the system herself. I feared that Sydney would not be so lucky.

That evening, after the house had quieted down from the day's activities, I headed downstairs to the library. The evening temperatures hovered around freezing, and the cold air threatened to come inside, if not for the wood heater we recently had installed into the basement, situated directly in front of my writing desk, where the old fireplace used to be. After stacking some more wood into it, I sat down at the desk and turned on the computer laptop. "Dear Lord," I began, silently praying to myself, "please lead me to Sydney, if this be Your will. Please help me to reach out to her and remind her that she is important to You and to us. Help me to find her. Amen."

Taking a sip of hot chocolate from the Donald Duck mug, I logged on to my Facebook account, the social networking site that reached millions across the globe. I then typed in Sydney's first and last name into the search bar at the top of the screen and was met with hundreds of people having the same name. As many of the names had a picture of that particular Sydney, I studied each, discounting many that were obviously not her and studying just as many others that possibly were. We had not seen our former foster child in six years, so I was unsure what she might look like now, at the age of 14. I then read through the profile of many of the Sydneys who would be around our Sydney's age. After an hour and a half of this, shoulders aching from hunching over the computer, I took a break and headed upstairs, getting Sydney's date of birth from Kelly and making another cup of hot chocolate. A quick roll of my shoulders in an attempt to ease the discomfort, and I was back in front of the computer, typing in Sydney's birth date next to her name on the social networking site. No luck; I found no Sydney that matched this date. I then typed in Alabama next to her name, as that is where we had heard she was last. Dozens of Sydneys from that state popped up on my screen, yet none were her. I then tried Georgia in the hope that perhaps she had made her way back to the state.

Two and a half more hours crept across the clock before I pushed my chair back from the writing desk and rubbed my eyes. My shoulders stung even more, and weariness was beginning to settle in. Stifling a yawn, I looked at the clock; it was close to midnight, and I had come no closer to finding her. Surely Sydney was out there somewhere. I had tried Facebook, internet searches, various child welfare agencies, but had only met with failure. Would I ever find her? Would she once again hear that her Daddy loved her?

* * *

The first day back to school after Christmas promised to be a memorable one. As it typically does, the first day back also landed on my birthday. This year, though, I was especially looking forward to Michigan State football game. This particular year, the team was playing in a championship bowl game against the University of Georgia, the team that many in our church and town cheered for. I had been hyping the game for the past few weeks; giving copies of Michigan State's fight song to several people throughout town, calling up others and singing the song to them over the phone, and wearing my team's green and white colors at every opportunity. I was looking forward to not only watching the game, but to celebrating my birthday with my family. As it was a teacher work day with no students at school, I was able to take half the day off, with the football game beginning at one that afternoon.

Arriving home a half hour before the game started, I walked into the house with anticipation. My Michigan State chair was already set up in front of the TV, and my favorite flavor of pizza and ice cream both awaited my birthday celebration. Before I could take five steps into the house, Jace met me, a look of concern written across her face. Normally, she was the calmest of all the children in our family; nothing seemed to faze her. Today, she was fazed.

"Daddy, Mommy says not to panic."

"Um, okay, Jace. I won't. Where is your mother?" I asked, looking around for a sign of my wife. I was ready to begin the birthday festivities. Jace's statement was an odd one, though, leaving me a little puzzled. Kolby, Brody, and Grace were standing alongside Jace, silent in their birthday greeting to me. This was the first time I had seen them all day long, and I had expected a bigger birthday hello from my children.

"Daddy, you need to get back in the car and drive to the hospital. Mommy had to take Myeisha to the emergency room."

"What?" I blurted out in a loud voice, not certain I heard her correctly. Hospital? Emergency room? I was completely unprepared for these words from my middle daughter. What did she mean I had to go to the hospital? Confused, I asked again, "Jace, what are you saying?"

"Myeisha had a seizure and Mommy had to call the hospital. An ambulance came to take them both away." The other children looked on, distressed, letting their sister take the lead. Kolby finally broke their silence, handing me the phone.

"Mommy says to call her, Daddy," the oldest child said.

Taking the phone from her, I dialed Kelly's number, but was met with her answering machine. This couldn't be happening, I thought. It was my birthday, I had my favorite meal ready for me, and I was looking forward to the football game. Instead, I grabbed Kelly's extra cell phone, told Kolby to watch the others, and dashed back out the house, all under an Olympic minute flat. As I started the car, I called Anne, leaving a message on her answering machine that Myeisha was in the emergency room and that I would call with more details later on.

A half hour later, I arrived at the hospital in a nearby city, as Monticello's hospital was too small to minister to such cases. It took me another half hour to track down Kelly and the small child in the hospital's waiting room area. Giving each a kiss on the cheek, I held the foster child in my arms while Kelly filled me on the details. Myeisha had been eating a snack in the high chair around ten that morning when Kelly and Jace noticed that she was kicking the chair and banging the top of the eating tray with her hands, a blank look upon her face. Trying to get her attention, Kelly noted that the foster child's face was pale. Quickly, my wife took the child out of the high chair, laying her down on a blanket, hoping to better examine her. Noting that she was completely unresponsive, my wife called her friend Shannon, our children's doctor, and reported Myeisha's condition. Without hesitation, Shannon strongly encouraged Kelly to call the emergency room. A half hour later, paramedics from the nearby city arrived in an ambulance and found that the child's fever had spiked to 105 degrees in a frighteningly rapid space of time. After giving her some medicine to reduce the fever, Kelly and her foster infant rode in the ambulance to the nearby city's emergency room. After bringing me up to date on the story, my wife collapsed in tears. Remaining calm throughout the ordeal, she now broke down into tears as the worry and anxiety overcame her. As I placed my arm around her, she quickly melted in my embrace. The uncertainty of the ordeal had been a terrifying one for her, and had exhausted her emotionally.

As we waited for a doctor to see her, I filled out the necessary paperwork. Like most foster children, we had little information on Myeisha, not even a social security number. So it came as quite a surprise when the secretary informed us that the child was already on record in their computer base. Our tiny foster infant had been in the hospital months before she came to live with us, though we were not given any information as to why. The waiting room was overflowing with scores of sick people. Chairs were filled by some while others lay on the floor or found refuge sitting in the corners of the room. New Year's must be a busy time of year for hospitals, I thought to myself as the three of us leaned against a wall. Forty-five minutes later, we were ushered into an emergency room by a nurse. In a matter of minutes, Myeisha was hooked up to a number of different machines, with wires and tubes coming out of her small frame, as the nurse tested her in a variety of ways. Quickly taking Kelly's hand, I placed my other upon our small foster child and began to pray aloud. "Heavenly Father, we are grateful for Myeisha in our lives, and are grateful for the opportunity to take care of this child of Yours. Please lead the nurse and doctors to what is wrong with her, giving them the wisdom to cure her of these seizures. Please also hold this tiny child in the palm of Your hand, washing over her with Your healing power. In Your name we ask, Amen."

During the next few hours, the nurse came and went, inserting a number of large needles into her small frame, needles that looked like something out of one of my favorite classic Frankenstein horror films from the 1930s and 1940s. Each time the nurse placed a needle into her, Myeisha would simply say, "No thank you," her voice barely registering over a whisper. No tears spilt forth from her during the next few hours, though there were many that were shed by my wife, as she looked on helplessly.

Once again, members of our church family had come to our rescue. Jace's friend, Sinclair, had called the house during the initial hours of the 2012 Birthday Event, as I had come to term it, asking if Jace could come over for the day. As girls often do, Jace shared the story with her friend, who then shared it with her mother, Hope. Without hesitation, Hope rushed to our aid, bringing Kelly and a large meal from one of the nearby restaurants, including an ice-cream shake for me, my birthday treat. Lynne and Steve had also heard of our dilemma, and soon began texting Kelly a play-by-play account of the football game. As her husband, Steve, was just as big a fan of the University of Georgia as I was for Michigan State, she was able to maintain a respectable and unbiased account of the game for me. As my wife read the texts to me over her phone, I interpreted back to her what each text meant, since my Australian bride knew nothing of the American sport. Three overtimes later, and after a game that went well over four hours, Michigan State prevailed, though I felt no joy over it. We still faced a wait in the hospital, as the doctor still was uncertain what the problem was.

It had been seven hours since we had first arrived into the emergency room. Myeisha was asleep, wires and tubes still attached to her. Numerous times the doctor and nurse had both come in and out of the room, checking various instruments, as well as the rate of her fever. By this time, the infant's temperature had reduced to 101 degrees, and a little color had come back into her face, though she still looked quite pale.

"I believe that your foster child suffered from a fever seizure," the young female doctor told us with a reassuring smile. "Her fever spiked so quickly, sending her into seizures."

"But, why did this happen?" I asked. "Does it have anything to do with the fact that she was born a drug baby?"

"It's hard to say," the doctor answered back. "It may be that, and it may happen again, but she should be okay now. I am a little concerned, though, about her fever still being just above one hundred. I would like you to take her to the children's hospital in Atlanta until her fever reduces."

I felt my shoulders tense at the thought. It had already been a long and emotionally exhausting birthday. I didn't enjoy the thought of it carrying any further into another hospital. Besides, I wasn't sure if the hospital had a birthday cake there with my name on it, or not. It was Kelly who spoke up; saving what was left of the day for us.

"My husband and I have four children of our own. We have been foster parents to dozens of others. I have a doctor's degree in nutrition. If I promise you that we will monitor her closely and take her to the hospital if she grows any worse, is there any way that we can just take her home with us now?" The exhaustion upon her face and weariness in her voice were unmistakable in my wife's plea; she was tired and simply wanted to go home. I imagine I looked the same to the doctor, as my birthday joy had long since left me; no "For he's a jolly good fella" tune was rolling off my tongue at that moment.

After a moment to consider, the doctor placed a hand on Myeisha and looked at us. "It may be against the hospital's policy, but I can tell that the two of you have been around the block or two with children, and know what you are doing. Yes, take her home, and watch over her. I think she will be okay in a day or two. Just promise me that you will call the moment she should relapse."

Thanking the doctor, Kelly and I then spent the next half hour filling out the necessary paperwork to release the child. Afterwards, we went around the hospital, thanking the nurses, doctors, and various staff who had helped us, including those who had prayed for Myeisha throughout her stay. Many of these nurses had come to visit us during the ordeal, having heard that we were foster parents to this tiny infant and being touched by her story. Finally, bundling her up in warm clothes and a heavy blanket provided by the hospital staff, Kelly and I walked out to the car, both finally able to release the tension and stress that the day had produced. For me, it had only been nine hours, but for my wife, it had been since the morning had begun. Yet, the tears for neither of us had stopped, as tears of joy flowed from both of us, anointing Myeisha further into our hearts.

* * *

"Did you hear that loud noise last night?" she asked me.

"No, I didn't hear a thing," I answered my wife as the two of us were getting dressed. The early February morning had seen the temperature become even colder, and the two of us were bundling up in warmer clothes. Grace, Brody, and Myeisha were at the table having breakfast while the two older girls were upstairs getting ready. Unfortunately for Brody and me, both Kolby and Jace had entered the age of long showers, hair curling, and the delicate art of choosing the right outfit for the day. This all meant that my son and I were forced into shorter showers and longer waits.

"There was a large booming sound, like something exploded," she responded as she slipped on the Australia wool sweater of hers.

"Hmmmm. Are you sure?" I was always a Doubting Thomas kind of guy, as I usually had to see something myself to believe it. This time, since I didn't hear any loud noise, I was skeptical. That was my first mistake.

"Yes," my wife said, her Australian accent thickened by the weariness of the early morning. "It was around two in the morning. It sounded like something blew up."

"Huh! I wonder what it was," I said, pulling on my own warm weather Michigan State sweater. The basketball team was playing this evening and, as usual, I had to wear something green to support my team. I was one of those fanatics, one of those face painters, obnoxiously painting my face green for important games. Tonight's game was against those pesky Wisconsin Badgers, a team that had given my Spartans quite a bit of trouble of late. After finishing breakfast, I kissed Kelly, Kolby, and Grace, and headed out the door with Myeisha in one hand, and my lunch in the other. Brody and Jace trailed behind, as I was working at the middle school.

My second mistake came ten minutes later as I drove into the day care to drop off Myeisha. Caught up in the anticipation of the basketball game later in the evening, as well as the general conversation with Brody and Jace, I completely ignored what would turn out to be rather significant to all of our lives. Instead, I dropped off Myeisha, and headed to the middle school, wished Brody and Jace a good day in their classes, and set to work for the day. It was Kelly, again, who brought the news to me.

"Boomie, did you see the house?" I could hear the anxiety in her voice on the other end of the phone. For the life of me, though, I had no idea what she meant.

"What house?"

"Myeisha's mother's house. The house she was staying at."

Taking a bite of the banana I had brought with me for lunch, I leaned against the counter in the work room of the library. "What's the matter with her house?"

"It blew up last night, and…"

Shocked by this bit of news, I interrupted her. "Blew up?" I had driven right past the house just a few hours earlier. How could I have missed this?

"Yes, the house blew up. I'm surprised you didn't see it. There is just a shell of it, now, as the whole house caught on fire. The roof is gone, and so are most of the walls. It's still smoking, and the trees around it are burnt from the heat and fire. Thank goodness Myeisha wasn't still living with her mom. Can you imagine?"

Both surprised and stunned, I feebly answered back, "Wow," before pausing to let it sink in. Kelly granted me a moment to process the information, as she knew full well that I needed the time. My next thought lay with the caseworker, Anne. It was important that she know, and since she did not live in town, the news might not reach her for a while. I thanked Kelly for calling, told her I loved her, and then called Anne. A few moments later, I hung up the phone with the caseworker, finished my lunch, and went back to work. It wasn't until another four hours had passed that I was able to see the full extent of the fire's damage to the house. As Myeisha's day care was located just next door, I drove slowly past the shell of a house. In fact, the damage was so extensive, it was difficult to recognize that it was a house. The white painted boards on the house were blackened by the flames, as if almost charcoaled themselves. The roof was gone, along with many of the walls. Before the fire, there had been a great deal of objects piled around the house; bikes, a grill, a weight-lifting set, rusted car, and numerous other items. Most were now gone, and what remained was difficult to recognize. I was relieved to hear earlier that morning from Kelly that no one was injured. Yet, where would Myeisha's mother now go to live? The answer would resurface in a significant way later on in the future and in all of our lives.

A week and a half later saw a different type of excitement come to our home. It was the Friday before Valentine's Day, and with it the annual Father Daughter Dance. This was the sixth year our church had hosted it, and it had become an event that many in the town eagerly looked forward to. I had read about another town hosting such an event roughly seven years ago, and had approached my church about holding one. The dance was a way to honor our daughters and granddaughters as gifts from God, as well as to teach them that they are to be treated by men with respect, dignity, class, and integrity. Since the inception of the dance six years back, it had grown each year, with more people from outside our church attending, as other fathers and daughters, and grandfathers and granddaughters from across the community had come to celebrate the life of these young ladies. This year promised to be the biggest yet, as

I had heard from a number of people in town that they were planning on coming.

The addition of Myeisha brought my total of girls attending to four, greatly outnumbering me. How was I to dance with each one? How was I to shower attention upon each princess in my family? Along with that, I wanted to spend time with each male who attended, making sure that those outside the church felt both comfortable and welcome. I felt like I was in charge of the Alamo, greatly outnumbered by forces. Fortunately, Kelly had made the suggestion a few months back to my parents, and I had reinforcements with the aid of my father, as he flew in from Michigan for the big night.

After work that Friday, I quickly drove to the florist to pick up the four corsages for the girls and the two boutonnieres for my father and me. As the church was just down the road from the florist, it was only a matter of a minute before I was inside the fellowship hall to make sure that the decorations and food were ready, and that the DJ and photographer were all set. Next, I made a mad dash back home, showered, and shaved. While putting on the tuxedo and Mickey Mouse bowtie, I shoveled some pizza down my throat, washing it down with a cold glass of milk. By this time, Kelly had helped the girls get dressed, curled hair, and sprinkled fairy dust on all of their faces, while my father patiently waited in the lounge room, taking in the circus-like atmosphere. It wasn't even an hour before I was back in the car, this time with four girls and my father, as we drove back to the church and to the arrival of the guests for that evening. Before long, the church fellowship hall was full of anxious girls and young ladies, nervous dads and granddads, and excited mothers, aunts, and grandmothers. As the crowd was so large, I asked Jamie to help me with the Grand March, the entrance and introduction of each couple. As Jamie, one of the local dentists in town and a fellow church member, had only one daughter, he was much more relaxed than I was, eager to help out.

A soft and peaceful song soon began playing over the DJ's two large amplifiers, indicating that we were to begin the night's festivities. Mothers, aunts, grandmothers, and a small collection of curious young boys, brothers of many of the dancers, soon gathered together on the far end of the fellowship hall, cameras and video recorders in hands and smiles on their faces. With microphone in hand, I introduced the first proud father and eager daughter by name, as they marched into the hall. Oohs and ahhs quickly were voiced by the ladies in attendance, and many hands were brought together in clapping. The father, dressed in a blue sport coat, pink tie, brown pants, and black dress shoes, tenderly held his daughter's hand in his left, as her own left encircled his right arm. The white full-length dress went down to her ankles, light pink shoes peeking out from underneath it, and a pink rose pinned to her dress accented the wide toothy smile of the seven-year-old. When the two stopped at the point I earlier indicated to all guests, dozens of cameras went off, while others held video recorders above their heads in an attempt to capture the moment. After a brief pause, the two moved on while another couple marched out, the mixture of nervousness and eagerness again being repeated in father and daughter. Soon, 40-some couples encircled the hall, as the line for those ready to march in dwindled to the remaining few. Handing the microphone over to Jamie, I rushed out of the fellowship hall into the adjoining hallway to find the girls and take my place in line. Soon, Kolby and Jace marched in on either arm of my father. While waiting, I looked down at Grace and Myeisha, both with smiles that if measured were probably half their size in weight. Four girls, I thought to myself with a smile. The joy I felt from my own three was hard to contain; the addition of Myeisha into the mix was a blessing, as I had come to love her as my own. Yet, I imagined that by this time next year, she would be gone; perhaps living with her mother, perhaps with Sue, perhaps with another family. How long would Myeisha be with us? How much longer would her smile brighten our home?

Chapter 10

Winter turned to spring in Monticello. Golden Forsythia waved their thin branches in the late March air, dogwood trees showcased their pink flowers, and daffodils danced in the breeze, just as the poet Wordsworth wrote. The air was filled with the sounds of tree frogs performing their mating song, newly hatched chickens cheeping in curiosity, and the tiny calls of newborn kittens in sanctuary under our porch. The evenings stretched out later, allowing me longer access to my garden beds. Pruning bushes, spreading mulch on flower beds, planting new flowers, and setting seeds into the cool soil were all jobs I tackled with enthusiasm. I found solace in the garden, as it allowed me time to reflect on the challenges of the moment, as well as to pray for wisdom and guidance for what lay ahead. It was a beautiful time of season, this time of rebirth and renewal. I was not aware, though, that Kelly wanted our own family to have a sense of rebirth, or at least of an addition.

"I think we should adopt Myeisha," my wife said to me as we headed to our foster parent association meeting that late March Thursday evening. I had known that my wife was feeling this way for some time, though she had yet to make it official by voicing it directly to me. I could feel her study me as I drove to the meeting, her eyes looking for a reaction from me.

Feeling the tension quickly mount in my shoulders, I tried to take a deep breath, before releasing it in a deep sigh. This was not a conversation to take lightly, yet one I knew was important to Kelly. Indeed, it was important to the future of this little girl. "I don't know" was all I could muster, as I truly didn't know where I felt on this topic. Though I had come to love her, I was by no means ready to take this step, adding a fifth child to the DeGarmo brood. The adoption of Grace a few years back was one I also was resistant to for a number of months. My initial belief with Grace was that our family had already been blessed with healthy children while there were others who were unable to have children of their own. I felt that the adoption of one more would have been a selfish act, and that the adoption of that foster baby would have been a blessing to another family. Yet, God had other plans, and He eventually opened my eyes and my heart to the adoption of Grace after 22 months as her foster parent. Our family was stronger for it, and I was a better person because of it.

"Boomie, she has come such a long way, and is such a part of our family. If she comes up for adoption, I can't let her go. It would not only break my heart, it would devastate her, as well. Can you imagine sending her to another home? She's so young, she would be so confused."

"I know, Kel," I responded. One of the many aspects that I loved and admired about my wife was her ability to love unconditionally all children who came into our home. Myeisha, though, had found a special place in her heart, and she was going to fight for her. "It's just that I don't know if I can do five children. Five children! Can you imagine? Think of the college bills; think of the weddings of four girls." I was exhausted just thinking about it.

"I know, but God will provide." Her reassuring smile and words of wisdom softened my stance a little. Still, five children seemed a daunting number to me. Perhaps I should have been watching the signs a little more closely, as God had bigger plans in store. Two weeks later, Kelly and I were hit with a bombshell that would again alter our family.

"Mom's pregnant again with a girl," Lisa announced to Kelly and me. Lisa had taken over as Myeisha's caseworker upon Anne's retirement. The three of us were sitting at the table in our parlor, holding our customary monthly meeting with the caseworker. The three older children were attending to homework while Grace and Myeisha played on the front porch, in full view of the three of us. We had been discussing Myeisha's progress, as well as the mother's. Myeisha's birth mother had found a home in a nearby township, moving back in with the birth father. Lisa had been telling us how the house the two were in was not one that DFCS would approve of if Myeisha were to return to the mother's care, as there were plumbing, electrical, and other housing problems. Along with this, the father was having a difficult time keeping a job, as he was in and out of jail, while the mother also had no steady income, either. By this time, Sue was no longer a viable option for Myeisha to return to, as the small child's former caretaker was not able to properly provide either.

"Really? When is she due?" Kelly asked for the two of us.

"She's due this July," the caseworker said, looking intently at us for a reaction.

"Same father?" I asked.

"Not really sure on that one," Lisa continued. I liked her frank and open attitude. Plus, she responded well to my jokes, which was an added bonus. "Mom says that the father is the same, while Myeisha's father says he isn't."

"Will this baby go into care also?" my wife wondered. It was her desire to keep the children together, if possible.

"Well, that's what I want to talk to you about," Lisa said. "We want to keep the two together."

"Would they both be up for adoption?" Did I hear her correctly? Did my wife just ask if two children were up for adoption? Surely, my ears had grossly played a joke on me. Either that or I had begun to lose my hearing at 43 years of age. She surely wasn't considering we adopt both.

"Yes, they would," said Lisa, with a smile.

"Great! I don't want to break the two of them up. Could we adopt them at the same time?" my wife asked.

Had she gone mad? Adopt two more children? This was insane! I was not at all prepared to become the next Brady Bunch family with six children on a permanent basis. Apparently, I needed to bring both Lisa and Kelly down to Earth. "Um, I'm not too sure about this," I said in a hushed tone, leaning over the table to emphasize my point. "I don't know if I can do six children now. I'm still not sure I want to do five children, and never said I was ready to adopt Myeisha."

Politely not addressing my comment, Kelly looked at Lisa. "Can we adopt one and not the other?"

"We want these two to stay together and go to the same home," the caseworker said.

I had to reassert myself into this conversation, as my first attempt at bringing some prudence to it was ignored. "You know what? I don't know that I want to do this," I said with an attempt at forcing a smile on my face. "We don't even know if this baby will be born healthy or not. She might have any number of problems or diseases. After all, her mother does not make the healthiest of choices. I just don't know, at this age, if I can take care of a child that has special needs. After all, there would be five other children to look after as well." There! Surely, this had brought some sagacity and wisdom back into this reckless conversation.

"My husband said the same type of thing when we first started talking about adopting Gracie as well; don't mind him too much. Can we take the baby in as a foster child when she goes into care?" my wife asked, abandoning me. I was adrift in this sea of conversation that was flowing around me.

"Yes, that can be done," Lisa replied. The next 20 minutes were then spent talking more about Myeisha's progress, though I heard very little of it. At some point, I subconsciously said I would attend the next court hearing for Myeisha, though I was not in complete control of my faculties at that point. My mind was still reeling from the idea of having six children call me "Daddy" on a permanent basis. After our meeting ended, we thanked Lisa for coming and headed back into the house. Kelly and I discussed the possibility of adopting another for a few more minutes before being called to parental duties with the other children. We did agree together that our family faced a situation that needed a great deal of prayer in the next few months.

The court hearing did come for Myeisha's permanency plan that second week of April. As I arrived at the historic and famous courthouse in our town, featured in many movies and television programs, I was met by Lisa who then introduced me to Myeisha's mother and father. I greeted each with a pleasant smile and hello, thanking each for coming. There was an uncomfortable air to our first meeting, as the mother's voice was barely audible in her response, not daring to look up. The father did look and thank me for taking care of his daughter, and then quickly looked down again. After telling them that it was nice to meet them, I entered into the smaller magistrate courtroom and waited for our foster child's case. Finding a seat towards the back of the courtroom, I watched as several other adults and children filed in, finding a seat themselves. It was quickly apparent that I was overdressed, wearing a suit and tie, while others around me were in jeans and t-shirts, the only exceptions being the caseworkers, lawyers, and courtroom employees. Recalling the last time I was in the courtroom to testify in Grace's parental termination, I began to feel a slight level of anxiety come over me. It's funny; I had performed in front of thousands in Up With People and pro-wrestling, and in front of countless numbers on TV in both venues, as well as working as a DJ in both the USA and Australia. At those times, I had never become nervous, yet here I was, in a small-town courtroom, simply observing a court hearing for a foster child, and I could feel the sweat begin to trickle down the back of my neck.

The majority of cases that morning dealt with children in foster care in the four surrounding counties, opening my eyes to a part of the foster care system that I was not truly familiar with and that disturbed me. The first case that morning saw a biological mother attempt to have her two small girls, aged seven and nine, move out of the foster care system. As the mother had moved to the nearby state of Alabama without informing DFCS and the caseworker, she wanted to bring the children with her. The judge felt otherwise, as the mother had not found a job and was unable to provide for her children. The judge also disciplined the mother, verbally scolding her for leaving the state unannounced, thus breaking part of the case plan assigned to her in order to gain custody of her children. Upset, the mother began screaming at the judge, lashing out at him in her own disappointment. I watched uncomfortably as her own children witnessed their mother's emotional outburst. What was even more troubling was watching the children say goodbye to their mother as they were leaving with their caseworker. The courtroom was filled with the sobs of both the grieving children and their unsettled mother, the children struggling to physically hold onto their mother while being pulled away by the child welfare caseworker. A troubled silence filled the courtroom for a moment when they finally left.

Following this case was that of a young mother who had to face charges of continued drug abuse while her children were in custody. Her child, a young boy around the age of ten, sat with both his caseworker and his foster parents, though I did not know either of them. The mother appeared disheveled, her clothing and hair unkempt and dirty. When she entered into the courtroom, her son quickly leapt up out of the cushioned pew, running into the arms of his waiting mother. Following behind him was his caseworker, and guided the two back to the seating area. As I observed the two of them converse, it became evident that the two had not seen each other for some time, laughing and carrying on in loud fashion. Soon after she came into the courtroom, the mother appeared in front of the judge, admitting that she had violated her case plan with the drug use. The judge was lenient on her, adding an additional six months to her one-year case plan. Again, I watched uneasily as the child listened to his mother's testimony. Like the case before her, the child broke into uncontrollable sobbing when it was time to leave, the brief reunion with his mother being interrupted with yet another forced separation from her.

The third case dealt with a mother whose rights to her own two-year-old girl were in the hands of the judge. After listening to the lawyers and caseworkers provide information and documentation on the mother's progress, along with the mother's testimony, the judge decided to terminate the rights of the mother and absent father based upon the fact that there was no evidence that the parents had implemented any of the steps of their case plan. Unlike the previous two cases, the mother simply hung her head, tears rolling down her prematurely aged face. The caseworker allowed her a few minutes with the two-year-old, who was oblivious to the decision. I imagined that the small child was not too familiar with her biological mother, as she had been in care for over a year, well over half her young life.

All three cases troubled me, leaving me disturbed. These children did not need to be in the courtroom during these hearings, I thought. I could only imagine that each of these foster children left the courtroom feeling even more afraid, even more confused, and even more alone than ever before. How could these children sit in a courtroom, in front of a judge and others, and watch their biological parents become upset without becoming upset themselves? Many times in the past, Kelly and I have had to pick up the pieces of emotionally distraught foster children when they returned to our home from court hearings. There were those times, too, when it seemed that our foster children had taken a step or three backwards from all the efforts Kelly and I had made with them. Too many times, we had found that birth parents had filled the children with false hopes about moving back home as well as false accusations about us. Watching these children today, screaming, kicking, and crying uncontrollably after watching their parents do the same, was most unsettling.

Three hours had passed since I first arrived in the courtroom, and there were several other cases heard by the magistrate and district judge, all involving children in some fashion. Throughout the process, I noticed that both Myeisha's biological mother and father were visibly stressed, and I could understand why. Any time one is to appear in court is unsettling, particularly if one's child is involved. From time to time during the three hours, the caseworker, Lisa, would walk over to where the two parents were sitting and speak to them in hushed tones while checking her watch at the same time. Finally, after another half hour had ticked off the courtroom clock, she came over to me, informing me that the court hearing would be postponed until the next month. The mother had hired a lawyer to represent her, even though DFCS would provide one for her at no cost. As the lawyer had not shown up for court, Lisa asked if the mother would like to have the services of the lawyer provided to her, but she declined. After making several unanswered calls to the hired lawyer, it was decided to wait until the next hearing the following month. Puzzled, I asked Lisa more about this. She quietly told me that this was an unusual request by the mother, as most parents do not hire a lawyer, due in large part to the cost involved.

Leaving the courthouse disappointed, I quickly got into my car and drove off to work. Driving past one of the local gas stations close to the courthouse, I noticed the mother and father standing outside, along with several others. The gas station was often frequented, both day and night, by those who were unemployed or others simply looking for a place to loiter. There were those occasions where I did not feel it was safe for Kelly to even pump gas from the establishment. As I drove past, a quick glance showed me that several outside the gas station, or petrol station as my Australia wife referred to it, were smoking, including the biological mother, pregnant with her unborn child, pregnant with the child I was asked to adopt. The danger of cigarette smoke to an unborn child was such common knowledge, I thought, yet this mother was selfishly ignoring it. The thought filled me with anger, as I considered it a crime against the helpless and fragile life she carried inside her. How dare this woman do this to her child? How dare she purposefully ruin this unborn child's health? My anger burned within me, fearing for this unborn child's future.

Yet, once again I was just as guilty myself. Recognizing my own judgmental attitude, I sent up a hasty prayer to God, asking Him to forgive me of my own sin of judging this lady. I was judging her on her actions, but I had done many things myself through the years that I was ashamed of. How could I get angry at her when God should be just as angry with me? Clearly, I had a long way to go in my Christian attitude.

The next month flew by quickly. May was upon us, and with it the last few weeks of school for the year. We had plans to travel to Australia with our four children to spend some time at Kelly's mother's house, and our Up With People reunion was taking place that summer as well, a reunion that my wife and I not only looked forward to, but were also hosting. Before the summer came, though, we had a great deal of things to attend to. The evenings saw me outside, busily working in the garden, attending to the new crops of veggies and fruits, as well as with the fresh flowers that were getting ready to burst out in bloom for the season.

The third week of May was particularly eventful. I returned to the courtroom on Wednesday morning, to attend another hearing for Myeisha. As we were seriously considering adopting the young one, Kelly and I felt that it was important for the court to see that we were fully involved with the child and her well-being. The morning proceeded much like the previous month's hearings, with many foster children being forced to watch their biological parents placed in a difficult situation, defending their actions to a judge. There was more crying, more parents breaking down as their children were pulled from them, more foster children grieving another separation. The scene was once again distressing, for all involved. I questioned why these children were brought to the court hearing, when instead they could be in the classroom, not only learning important school information, but also avoiding these emotional horrors.

Like the previous month, the hired lawyer was not present to represent the mother. Lisa once again gave her the option to be represented by the court-appointed attorney, yet Myeisha's mother refused. Relaying this information to me in the back of the courtroom where I was seated, she told me that June's court hearing would go differently, as the mother would not be permitted to have an attorney represent her. Two failed attempts had apparently been enough for both the caseworker and the judge; she would be represented by the court-appointed lawyer, whether she desired this or not. Disappointed that I once again missed half of my work day in the courtroom for something that did not transpire as planned, I quickly let Lisa know that I would not be able to make the June hearing, as I would be in Australia. Driving back to work, I went over in my mind the events of the morning, and of those that lay ahead the next night; the foster parent association meeting. These meetings were ones that I looked forward to, as they allowed Kelly and I to relax with other foster parents and were generally stress free, usually holding no surprises for us. Little did I know that this next meeting would not only break this pattern, but the surprise it held would potentially forever alter our family.

* * *

"Dinner was great, Lynne. I can't begin to tell you what a treat this is for us." Standing over the sink in the church kitchen, I washed the plate and handed it to Lynne. A few months back, she had approached me about how she might be able to do her part helping foster children. Our conversation led to this evening, dinner and child care provided for the foster parents in our county during our foster parent association meeting. Lynne, along with a few other members in our church, had organized the foster parent support group, and the results were exceptional. Kelly, I, and our fellow foster parents could sit down together to a home-cooked meal and relax while others looked after the children. It was the closest thing to going to a restaurant without children that Kelly and I and the other foster parents had experienced in a very long time, a strange kind of date night.

"I'm glad I can help. Steve and I can't be foster parents, so we try to help you and the others this way," she responded with a smile. "How are things going with Myeisha's case? Do you think you will be able to keep her?" Like Grace before her, there were many in our church that were hopeful that this young child would stay with us, as we had become the only family she truly knew.

"Yes, I think it's going to happen," I said. For the first time, I became excited about the idea of adopting the small child, and had a difficult time repressing the grin that was forcing itself across my face. "We've been told that we should expect it to happen sometime soon. In fact, Kelly and I are now calling her 'Brailey,' a name Kelly chose."

"That's wonderful!" Lynne replied. "I'm so happy for her. Now, you let me clean up in here, and you get back to your meeting." As she ushered me out, I thanked her again for the dinner and returned to the church's fellowship hall, helping to clear the rest of the dishes in order to begin the meeting and training session.

An hour and a half later, Kelly and I were saying our goodbyes to the other foster parents and getting ready to head home for the evening. As we were finishing with the last of the cleaning, Lisa came up to the two of us, a look of distress slightly creasing her forehead. "John and Kelly, I have some news for you about Myeisha."

"What is it?" my wife asked in a cheery manner. She, too, had enjoyed the evening and was in good spirits.

"It looks like Myeisha may go to live with a relative soon," the caseworker answered, looking at Kelly from across the small table that separated the three of us.

Her news hit me like a jackhammer, suddenly knocking all joy from me, leaving me struggling for breath. I heard Kelly gasp, also, as she placed her hand upon my arm, clenching it in a vice-like grip. In her shock, her nails dug into my skin, bringing a second type of pain and discomfort to me. I quickly gathered myself, asking, "What do you mean? I thought that was all behind us!"

"There is an aunt who is hoping to take Myeisha into her home. That's all the information I have for you at this time," Lisa said with empathy.

Visibly upset by the news that Myeisha might leave our home, Kelly took a deep breath before asking, "Will you let us know as soon as you can?"

"Of course," Lisa replied. "I know this is hard news for you, but sometimes it happens. Thank you for all you have done for Myeisha; she's in a great home, and I can tell that she is loved and cared for."

We thanked Lisa for the kind words, said our goodnights, and headed for the car. As I drove home, Lisa's words continued to ring in my ears. The thought of Myeisha leaving to live with someone that she did not know well, if at all, left my stomach in knots. Indeed, it felt like someone had punched me in the gut. By the time we had arrived home, it was well past the bedtimes of Grace and Myeisha, and Brody, Jace, and Kolby were not too far behind them. Kelly and I soon had the small ones in bed, and said our goodnights to the older ones. Kolby and Jace began working on their school work, while Brody was nose deep in a book. The house was soon quiet, with one exception, the sound of Kelly's crying.

For the first time, when Kelly looked at me, through a tear-drenched face, and told me that she was through fostering, I did not have the strength to encourage her, as I silently agreed with my wife. She has said this for years, though I always encouraged otherwise. This time, I didn't know, and the thought of that alone disturbed me. My heart was broken at this strong possibility that Myeisha would go and live in another home, a home that might not provide the best for her. The argument was that this was her family. I had seen that argument fail too many times. Children do not necessarily need their family; they need the best possible chance for them to survive and succeed in a loving family. A biological family did not necessarily mean a child would succeed. I only had to look at our beloved and adopted Grace as an example.

To be sure, I understood it was part of the process of being a foster parent. We had experienced this before with Sydney, who stayed with us for a year and a half before moving to live with an aunt and uncle, family members who adopted her. That did not go well, sadly, and she was now back in foster care in another state. Her family failed her at numerous occasions. Going back to her family was a complete failure for her, and has perhaps damaged her beyond care. Try as I might to track her down, I had not had luck. I could not bear to repeat this with another child.

As I turned into bed that night, Myeisha's situation left me sleepless. In her grief and sadness, Kelly cried herself to sleep, while I lay in the bed, unable to sleep myself. Incapable of escaping the worry and anxiety that left a gnawing pain in my stomach and tension in my head, neck, and shoulders, my mind wandered throughout much of the night and into the wee hours of the morning. I was disturbed that DFCS was considering placing the small child with a family member, one who had not even stepped up for the past 11 months, a third of Myeisha's life. This child had come to know our family as her only family. Placing her in yet another strange house, albeit a biological family, would cause undue stress and anxiety upon the young foster child.

Will Myeisha have as much love in this new house, I wondered. She was surrounded by love in our house, with two supportive parents, and four siblings who dote on her. Will she have as much stability in this new house? Kelly and I both held down two stable jobs, providing stability for our children in many ways. Will she experience as many possibilities and opportunities in this new house? We just took our children to Europe, and are heading off to Australia. Experiences like this are once in a life time, and offer untold educational opportunities and life lessons. I wanted Myeisha to see a world of possibilities outside Monticello, just like my own children. What worried me was that if I did not fight for her hard enough now, at this very moment, not only would she not have these experiences and opportunities, but I feared I would one day soon have to face her in a store in town, or even in school, a child in need.

The past year and a half has seen nine foster children in my home, some with very difficult challenges placed upon them and upon Kelly and me. I was tired. More than that; I was exhausted. Initially, when we came back from Europe, we had planned on a break. Yet, as is often the case, God had other plans for us, and we took this little one in. Despite all my better judgment, knowledge, and experience as a foster parent telling me otherwise, we began to believe that Myeisha would become part of our family forever. Kelly had even begun to believe that perhaps we would take in her unborn sibling, as well, and have the blessing of raising that child, though I was unsure of this myself.

I was disappointed in the system, as I had seen failure in many parts. Too many children had gone back to homes that were not healthy, that were not stable, and, in some cases, homes that were not safe. While I did not know this new aunt who wanted to adopt her, I did not wish to see Myeisha end up like Sydney, right here in the town I lived in, and be powerless to help. Yet, if she left our home, for the first time I wasn't sure if she would be the last foster child to leave our home. Maybe if she went, after ten years of fostering I would be done as well. Perhaps my heart simply could not take this any more.

Chapter 11

One of the challenges that Kelly and I faced in an international marriage was that of family. Wherever we lived, at least one of us would be far from our parents, cousins, grandparents, and extended family. Though my own parents lived 18 hours away by car, we considered that very close, considering Kelly's mother and family were in Australia. My parents lived on the same continent, even the same hemisphere, while Kelly's lived half a world away, in a different hemisphere, on a different continent, on the other side of the world. In fact, the two places couldn't be much further apart.

Besides the great distance that separated the two sets of families was also the great expense. As Myeisha was not allowed to travel outside of the state, a trip to Australia was certainly out of the question, and she went to stay with another foster family who provided respite care for us. With our four children, plus Kelly and I flying, the price was well over ten thousand dollars for tickets alone, a steep price for one on a teacher's salary, and a price that was well beyond our means. Thankfully, a friend of the family worked at an airline, and was able to give us "buddy passes," allowing us to fly for only the cost of the tax. The only drawback was that we would ride "standby," meaning we were not guaranteed a seat on a particular flight, but on the next flight with empty seats.

This drawback became more of an obstacle on the way to Kelly's mother's house in the Land Down Under. We were able to make the flight from Atlanta to Los Angeles just fine, arriving in the City of Angels that first Friday in June. Yet, the ten p.m. flight to Sydney, Australia, was full, leaving us stranded in the airport. As the next flight did not leave until ten that next evening, the six of us simply found a quiet corner of the busy airport and tried to sleep. Kolby, Jace, Brody, and Grace were all troopers, with nary a complaint, taking the cancelled flight and sleeping arrangements all in their stride. Fortunately, we were able to board the next flight, 24 hours later, finally arriving at Shirley's house 52 hours after we initially left.

The three weeks in Kelly's home town of Dubbo, located in the state of New South Wales, went by quickly, and soon we found ourselves heading back home. If we thought the flight over was a long one, we were mistaken, as we were hit a second time by the aviation plague of "standby." Once again, we found ourselves stranded in Los Angeles, our old airport nemesis, as the flights from the Californian city to Atlanta were full. This time, though, there were numerous flights back to the capital city of Georgia, instead of the one flight to Kelly's homeland that we encountered before, giving us many more opportunities to make it back home. At least, that was Kelly's and my initial thought when we found ourselves once again trying to sleep in the airport. Both of us concluded that we would be able to catch the next flight home. When that didn't happen, there was the next one, and the next, and then the next. Surely we would be able to get a flight home. After all, it was only a three-hour flight from Los Angles to Atlanta, so very close. But it wasn't close at all; it ended up being so very far instead. Forty-eight hours later, we were still unable to acquire any standby seats. At one point, after spending the night in the airport two nights in a row, I began to think my children, wife, and I were in the middle of a movie. Desperate, Kelly and I gave up on the miracle of "standby," purchasing tickets to make the short trip home. The entire 78-hour trip from Kelly's old

Australian home to our bungalow in Monticello was one that convinced me that "standby" was not part of the friendly skies for my family. Seventy-eight hours; I might as well have been traveling between the two continents by boat.

Four days after we arrived home, Kelly and I sat in the parlor for our monthly meeting with Lisa. The caseworker was listening to Kelly explain how Myeisha seemed very happy to see us after our vacation. The little one had stayed with another foster family during the time, and our initial concern was that she might not remember us. She proved us wrong when she ran up to me, squeezing me in an embrace that was well beyond her two-and-a-half-year small frame, when I had arrived three days beforehand to pick her up. Her squeals of laughter and joy upon seeing Kelly and the children when we arrived home were additional proof that she not only remembered us, but also missed us. Our family of seven was back together. Plus, we had another addition as well. Just the day before our meeting with Lisa, we had taken in Chiara, a 14-year-old from Switzerland. Chiara's parents were friends with Connie and Hans, and the young teenage girl had come to spend the summer with us in hopes of seeing what life was like in the United States. Close in age to Jace and Kolby, the young Swiss teenager had not only fitted right in with those two, but had instantly connected with Brody and Grace, as well. For Kelly and me, we were pleased not only to allow Chiara an opportunity to see what life was like in America, but we were also happy for the chance for our own children to learn some of the Swiss German language from our newest house resident.

After watching Myeisha interact with us, Lisa was pleased to see that the foster child was well. The caseworker also brought us news that the plans for the aunt to take in the child had fallen through during our overseas excursion, resulting in our family being at the top of the list again, so to speak, to adopt the young one. I was hesitant, still unsure if that was truly God's plan. Plus, I knew full well that there were many hurdles ahead in this adoption process of a foster child, as there was still possibly other biological family members who may want her. Along with this, there was also the strong chance that the biological parents would be able to be reunited with her. Addressing these concerns to Lisa, she again broached the idea of the adoption of the unborn child.

"Dr. DeGarmo, I very much appreciate your concerns," the caseworker said to me. Taking another sip from the homemade lemonade in her hand, she lifted Myeisha off her lap and unto the floor. Kelly motioned for the lightly brown-skinned child to go outside and join Grace and Brody, who were playing with the football in the front yard. "The mother will not be able to have custody of her newborn child, though, as she is in no condition to look after a baby. In fact, DFCS will move for termination of the parental rights soon on the baby, and we will try to move for termination on Myeisha, at the same time. We really wish to have these two stay together."

While Kelly was again excited about this possibility, the idea of adopting two more children unsettled me, and I told Lisa and Kelly as much. With the baby coming in July, our house would be full; too full, I thought. Not only did we already have six children, with the addition of Chiara, but we also had a number of visitors coming early to our house before the mid July Up With People reunion that Kelly and I were hosting in the Georgia mountains. I simply wasn't sure that I was up to taking in another baby again.

Placing my glass of water down, I tried to explain my thoughts and concerns to both the caseworker and my wife. "Lisa, I just don't know if I can do this. I have been changing diapers now for 14 years straight, without a break. I don't really want to do this anymore. With a baby, we would be starting all over again, from scratch. The thought of that exhausts me. Plus, I would be…"—I then paused for a few seconds in order to properly calculate in my head before going on—"…well, I would be around 62 when this baby graduates from high school. At that rate, I would never be able to retire!" The last sentence came out of me in near hysterics, as I tried to laugh it off. Unfortunately, my laughter rang out a little too maniacally.

My sanity was slipping away from me at even the thought of working myself into the grave.

Minutes later, after my brief excursion into the world of hysteria, we bid Lisa farewell. Kissing Kelly on the cheek, I drove off myself to run some errands, including a trip to the local grocery store, as our house was still barren since returning from our vacation of the food and diapers necessary for a house full of eight people. As Monticello was a little town, each of my destinations was quite close to each other in proximity. This is part of the charm of the town. Another one of the charms is that everyone seems to know everyone else, as the population is so very small. Unfortunately, this was not quite so charming when it came to being a foster parent to children from the quaint rural countryside town. We found when we fostered Grace that we would often come into contact with biological family members and friends of the family in venues such as the grocery store, bank, and even the public library, making for uncomfortable encounters. On this day, I was to experience yet another one of these encounters, this time with Myeisha's birth father.

"Hey John, is that Myeisha in the car?" I heard while pumping gas. The little one and Grace were both in the car with me, giving Kelly an opportunity to spend time with the older children. Turning around from the gas pump, I found Myeisha's father peering through the window.

"Umm, yes it is," I replied, feeling a little uneasy.

"How she be doin?" he asked, with a smile on his face.

"She's doing very well, thank you."

"Great!" he replied, with sincerity in his voice. When I had last met him, at the courthouse a few months back, he had been polite, thanking me for taking care of his child. Still, I was a little wary, due to my experiences in the past with some birth family members who lashed out at Kelly and I in anger. His next question did not help to put me at ease. "Hey, ya got some money I kin barrah?"

Inching closer to the car, I quickly answered, "No, I am afraid I don't." This was awkward, I thought. Why wouldn't the gas pump go any faster?

"Need yur lawn mowed? I kin mow yur lawn fur ya," he shot back in persistence, again with a smile on his face.

"No, I've got it, thank you."

"Yeah, but I kin come on ovah to yur house and do it. You kin jest rest." He was determined, it seemed, to get me to agree to his offer.

"Well, I really enjoy doing it," I tried to reassure him. "Besides, I need the exercise if I want to stay in shape." With this, I finished pumping the gas and said goodbye. Driving off, I was happy to get away from the uncomfortable encounter. As I drove away, I was struck by the fact that this type of encounter between foster parents and biological parents would be rare, if not unheard of, in larger cities, such as Atlanta. Yet, not one minute later, as I drove past the town's post office a few blocks away from the gas station, I passed Grace's biological grandmother as she walked down the street. Two children displaced from their homes due to issues beyond their control; two children in need, unable to return to their biological families; two children from the same town, and living in my home, as part of my family. I found it ironic that I would speak with one and drive past the other within minutes. Was Mayberry like this?

* * *

It was four that afternoon when the phone rang. Shannon was standing next to me in the kitchen, while Kelly was poolside with some of the early arrivals for our reunion. Connie and Hans had come early from Germany, along with some others from across the United States. As Shannon was closer to the phone, I asked her to get it. "Boom, it's for you," she said, handing me the phone.

"Hello," I said, taking the phone in my hand.

"Hello, John." The voice on the other end was instantly recognizable, and sent me into a near panic attack. Surely, this was not the Call for the baby.

"No! No, no, no, no, no!" I responded. Perhaps it was a panic attack I was having.

"John, please put Kelly on the phone."

"No! This can't be happening! It's not time! It's so not the time! Not today!"

Shannon stood back, either to watch me lose it, or to laugh in hysterics; I wasn't sure.

"I'm afraid so, John. The baby was born today. Are you ready?" the caseworker asked.

"This is not the time!" I strongly suggested once again. "Put the baby back in!" I shouted. By this time, I had certifiably lost it. I had lost my senses, and was putting on a display of lunacy to anyone within ear shot of me. "We have 70 people coming from around the world tomorrow, for a big reunion. We have been planning this for a year. Isn't there any way you can postpone this?"

"I'm sorry, John, but the baby is already out." I could hear Lisa laughing on the other end of the line. While she saw some humor in the situation, I certainly did not. "Is Kelly there?"

"Yes, she's on her way," I replied, as Shannon went outside to the pool to get her. "Listen, is there any way you can keep the baby in the hospital until we get back? We just can't take her right now." After all, I thought, it was quite normal for mothers and babies to stay in the hospital for a number of days in Australia; perhaps this hospital could make an exception.

"No, I'm afraid not. The baby will probably be released in the next day or so."

"Well, is there another family that could take this baby in, just until we return?" First I was in denial, now I was in the bargaining phase. I was clearly an emotional wreck.

As Lisa began to explain that this was not a possibility, Kelly walked into the kitchen, excited from the news that Shannon shared with her. I quickly said goodbye to Lisa, explaining that my better side was here to talk with her. In this case, Kelly was clearly, without a shadow of a doubt, 110 percent, my better side, as the side I was putting on was not real pretty at the moment.

"Okay, let me ask John and I'll call you back," I heard Kelly say, snapping me back from the twilight zone I was clearly in. "She wants to know if we are ready to take this baby in," my wife said, motioning me to follow her into the bedroom.

"Kelly, I know I've said this before, but I just don't know. This is big, and…" My voice trailed off, as I was unable to find the words to express the myriad of emotions that were swirling inside of me.

"Let's say a quick prayer before I call Lisa back," my wife suggested.

Taking her hands in mine, I began. "Dear Lord, thank you for this opportunity to serve You. We don't know what to do in this situation, and look to You for guidance. Please give us some kind of sign what we should do with this tiny baby. In Your name we pray. Amen." Finishing the prayer, I looked at Kelly, asking, "Well, what do you think we should do? This is a big step for us."

"Boomie, I think this is the perfect time to take this baby in. After all, we are surrounded by our best friends from all over the world. What could be a better time?" she asked, looking at me with a reassuring smile.

"You're right," I said, giving her a kiss on the cheek. "You're absolutely right." We then headed out back towards the pool, and broke the news to our own children, as well as to our friends. Our own four children were excited at the possibility of another sister, while our friends congratulated us on our bravery, and our commitment.

The next morning found me on the front porch with Skip, an Uppie who had traveled from the Ukraine for the reunion. We had just finished getting the coolers, food, drinks, and other items packed into the car, and were taking a moment to relax. I had calmed down, greatly, since my near panic attack the day before. It had been 20 years since I had seen Skip, yet it only seemed days. His adventures had taken him across the world and back, countless times, yet he remarked that he was in awe of what Kelly and I were about to undertake. "Boomer, I don't know how you do it. You sit here, so relaxed, yet you're about to have a baby delivered to your house. I'd be freaking out. This is a major thing that's about to happen. How are you doing it?"

With a straight face, I looked across at my friend, and simply said, "Heavy drugs." After the laughter died down, I thought I'd better clear the air, lest any suspicion linger. "Actually, Skip, we have been doing this for so long, that it really isn't too big of a deal. We have had so many children come and go, that you kinda get used to it after a while. It's kind of our norm, if that makes any sense." After a few more minutes of conversation, the two of us headed back inside as it was time for our caravan of five vehicles full of Uppies and children to depart on its two-hour journey to the resort that we had rented for the summer's reunion.

The afternoon was a whirlwind of activity and excitement as friends from across the globe gathered together, some for the first time in over 20 years. Many of them brought their own children with them, and our own children, plus Chiara, were able to make new friends from different parts of the world. That first night, Thursday, we were in the middle of a slide-show presentation of our year on the road, traveling and performing with Up With People, when Kelly got a phone call from Lisa; the baby was on its way. Pulling me aside, Kelly whispered to me that she didn't want to create a big scene, but instead wanted to do the placement quietly. Placement; I still had a hard time believing that we were going to have a foster child, a day-old baby, placed with us while we were far from our house for the next several days. Good thing Brian and Hans, two pediatricians, were with us. Our 27-hour-old foster baby now had two baby doctors from two different continents waiting upon her.

It was ten p.m. when Lisa's car pulled up. As the resort was tucked away in the northern Georgia mountains, we were surrounded by forests, making it quite difficult to see in the dark of the night. Add to this the lack of lighting on the outside of the resort building, and it was most dark, indeed. Lisa was able to find us from the dim light of Kelly's cell phone, which she waved above her head as a signal. We met Lisa as she got out of the car, walking to the other side of the vehicle, where the newborn was sitting in the back seat. Opening the rear door of the car, I was surprised when an adult face smiled back at me; Lisa had brought her mother along with her, as the drive was far for her, and it was late at night. Without any word of encouragement, Kelly unbuckled the tiny baby, and gently took her out of the car. The emotion of the moment brought tears to her eyes, while Lisa simply looked on, smiling. After a moment, my wife handed the fragile newborn to me. Studying it, I noticed that the baby's skin color looked quite…well, it looked quite pinkish; kind of like mine and Kelly's. As we were told that the baby's father was the same as Myeisha's, this was confusing. Remembering an old Up With People song in my mind, I looked at Lisa with a smile, asking, "So, what color is God's skin? Is it black, brown, yellow, red or white?" Perhaps it was the emotion of the moment, but for once, my wife laughed at one of my jokes.

"What's her name?" my wife asked, anxious to call the baby anything other than "the baby."

"Well, I'm not quite sure," the tired caseworker said. "Mom is calling it one thing, yet the spelling of it is something different than how it's pronounced."

"Well, that's okay," my wife responded. "She's simply precious."

Lisa handed over to us a few bottles, diapers, baby wipes, baby clothes, and formula to last us a few days, along with a baby car seat. Kelly and I had prepared the day before and had brought with us a portable crib.

As it was rather late at night, coupled with the fact that she had a long drive ahead of her in the dark, Lisa prepared to bid us farewell. Placing a hand on Kelly's shoulder, her smile dropped just a little. "I do have to tell you that there is a chance that the baby has chlamydia from her mother. We can do some tests on her next week; just keep on eye on her." Chlamydia: a sexually transmitted disease that could possibly cause this baby, this tiny innocent baby, to go blind. Once again, the sins of a parent were reaching out to grab a hold of a child, and the thought of this innocent child being affected angered me, though just for a moment. Looking at my wife smiling at the newborn snapped me out of the momentary judgmental feelings I was harboring within me.

"Okay, we'll see you next week," Lisa said, as she walked around her car, getting in behind the steering wheel.

"Wait, don't we have to sign all the normal paperwork for this child?" I asked, puzzled.

"No, we can take care of that when you're done with your reunion. Besides," she said, with a weary grin breaking forth from the corners of her lips, "we know where you live."

This was a first for me. In all my years of fostering, I was surprised by the fact that we didn't have to sit through an hour or so of signing paperwork and documents. Yet, in no way was I complaining, as I was anxious to get back inside to our friends, as well as to share the newest addition of the clan with our own children.

When we re-entered the lodge, we were met by 70 people, both children and adults, all waiting anxiously to see the newest arrival. Apparently, Hans had a window view, watching Kelly and my rendezvous with Lisa and the baby, and had shared the news with the others. The others quickly surrounded us, and the room was suddenly filled with tears, the baby's arrival striking an emotional chord for all gathered. After a word of encouragement from Kelly, Kolby and Jace ran upstairs to wake up Grace and Myeisha, as she wished to have the entire family not only together, but wanted our oldest foster child to meet the youngest foster child, her newborn sister. Making their way through the crowd, our adopted daughter and foster daughter were soon by our side, rubbing the sleep out of their eyes. Holding the baby in one hand, Kelly bent down to the two-and-a-half-year-old's level and took her hand. "Myeisha, Honey, this is your new sister."

Without hesitation, Myeisha kissed the tiny infant on the forehead. "Hello," she said. For the past 20 minutes, I had successfully held it in, kept my emotions in check, and had not shed a tear. Yet, this kiss, this simple kiss from one sister to another, opened up the floodgates within me, as the tears began to flow freely from me. It was at that instant, looking around at the friends who had traveled across the globe to join us, all with their own tears in their eyes, that I realized what Kelly had realized months ago. God's call for us was to adopt both of these young girls; our family was to grow by two more, and I had no reservations about it. He had surrounded us with so many who loved us, and had been with us since we first met, and who were now with us during this important time of change within our family. Indeed, God's timing was perfect, and I could clearly see it at this moment. Unabashedly, I let the tears fall where they may, and there were a lot of them. Indeed, I may have soaked the carpet around me, as the tears that flowed freely from me were so bountiful.

The next several minutes saw many of our friends press close to take a picture of the newborn child, as well as to get a better glimpse of her. As the noise level was rather loud, Brian stepped over to Kelly's side. Placing an arm around her, the pediatrician smiled and said, "As one of the baby's official foster doctors, I think she might need to get some sleep." Taking his cue, Kelly excused herself from the crowd and headed out of the room. Before she made her way to our bedroom, she headed back upstairs, to where Ed was waiting. Ed had long ago lost the use of both of his legs to an accident and had been confined to a wheelchair for much of his life, including the year we traveled with him. Not wanting to disturb the others by asking for assistance down to the ground level of the lodge, where the others were, he simply faded into the background, as he often did, calmly waiting for the excitement to die down. My wife would have none of it, though, and took the tiny seven-pound infant to him, allowing him to hold her. Ed was clearly touched not only by the opportunity to hold the child, but also by Kelly's gesture. Afterwards, she took the baby to the bedroom and gave it a bath before putting it to bed.

"Boomie, what are we going to call this child?" she asked me, as I finished tucking Myeisha into her own portable crib, and Grace into her bed. We were fortunate that the bedroom we had was big enough to hold two cribs, and two beds, as it had abruptly become Baby Central. "Shannon's daughter, Bethany, suggested Chasity. What do you think?"

"Hmmm, that's a tough one," I replied. In the past, Kelly and I had always had a difficult time coming up with a name for a child. For our own children, we had plenty of time to consider it, practicing different names and suggesting others. With Grace and Myeisha, the two had come to us as foster children, already attached with a name given to them by their mothers. With both, we had plenty of time for names during the adoption process. Yet, this little one was in desperate need of a name, one that we could pronounce to begin with, and one that would fit her as part of our family. After all, the now 31-hour-old child was, according to DFCS, to have parental rights terminated in the near future. "Well, Bethany suggested 'Chasity,' because it sounded like Cast E," I said. During our year traveling with Up With People, there were five casts, A to E, performing across the globe. "Since we have many people from Cast E here with us, and since you and I both met in Cast E, how about we change Chasity to Cassie? It kinda sounds like Cast E."

My wife smiled at the thought. "I like it," she said. "What do you think, little one? Do you like the name 'Cassie'?" she asked, kissing the baby on the forehead as she began feeding the little one a bottle. "Okay, Cassie it is." Kelly smiled back at me.

The next day saw 30-some children from across the nation quickly become friends, with Myeisha tagging along behind them. Cassie went from one comforting arm to another, as there was no shortage of people who wanted to shower the tiny foster child with love. Throughout the day, everyone had an eye on Kelly and me, along with Cassie to make sure that there was never a time that went by without the exact amount of help and support. Her plight had deeply affected those attending the reunion, and many rushed out to nearby stores to buy her clothing and other items. Dave from Washington accompanied me on a trip to buy Cassie some formula and diapers. As I knelt down at the bottom shelf, looking over the various kinds of baby formula, I noticed Dave from the side formula aisle, staring down at me in a confused grin. "How do you know what to get, what to do?" he asked.

"It's not too hard, after you do it a while," I answered with a laugh.

"If you asked me to go into a store and buy things for a car or motorcycle, or just about anything else, I could fake it and figure it out. But this? Not a chance. I wouldn't know where to begin." I chuckled at this. Yet, at the same time, I was struck with the realization that some of my friends lived a completely different lifestyle than I. Kelly and I had devoted our lives to taking care of children in need, while many others in society simply did not appreciate the daily trials and tragedies that foster children went through.

It was later that evening when Joe came up to me. From Minnesota, Joe was one of my dear friends from the year we traveled, and it was great to see him. Joe had recently finished studying to become a Unitarian minister, though he was currently working in an information technology job in Colorado. "Boom, would you mind if I gave Cassie her first blessing?" he asked me, with tenderness in his voice that immediately captured my attention.

"Absolutely, Joe," I answered. "I would be most honored." I was touched by his gesture. We were standing next to Shannon, who was holding Cassie at the time, with Kelly in the nearby room. I quickly told her about Joe's request, and she joined us, along with a host of others.

"Here you go," Shannon said to Kelly, trying to hand the newborn over to her foster mother.

"No, she's just fine," my wife said, a warm smile spread across her face. "She's in the perfect spot with you." Tears quickly appeared in Shannon's eyes by Kelly's gesture, as she had expected my wife would want to hold the baby for the event. Instead, Kelly was happier sharing the moment with others.

Surrounded by Kelly and me, along with the other Uppies, Joe placed his hand upon the tiny child. "Little one, what an amazing blessing your arrival is for all of us here," he began. "We came from across the world, old friendships that have remained timeless, bound together by our youthful optimism that together we really could make the world a better place in our small way. And now, decades later, the gift of your presence has reminded us all of why we were all drawn to that idea of Up With People in the first place. Seeing you here, just days old and knowing the love you will receive from your foster family and our Love for both of them is no coincidence. It is a reminder to us that faith, no matter the source of our individual beliefs, is what brought us together so many years ago. Faith in others, faith in love, faith in life. The Big Universe brought us all together through purpose and meaning. That which brings all things into existence."

"And all the love that is before you now is the Big Universe telling you that all of these people here before you have been called together to offer you their blessing. The spirit of this community of friends and the blessing we share with you and the blessing you have shared with us is your introduction into this amazing life. All of the possibilities of the world have been granted to you. Remember this blessing of love throughout your life and we will remember the blessing of you. You were meant to be."

As he finished, the others surrounding the child each kissed her on the forehead, their own faces filled with the emotion of this sudden and unexpected moment. Indeed, none of them had even considered the possibility that they would have a newborn baby delivered into the midst of them, into the middle of the reunion, let alone a child in need. Wiping away his own tears, Joe gave Kelly and me each a hug. Placing the baby into bed, we joined the others, as the tears soon broke way to laughter, late into the wee hours of the morning.

It was Sunday when I had a chance to speak to Joe one on one about the blessing. He had accompanied me on the hour-long drive, as I delivered Jace and Brody to the week-long church choir camp. This was the first time in several years I had not joined them, serving as a counselor and drama teacher for the gathering of youth from the central area of the state. Asking him his thoughts about the entire Cassie episode, he thought a moment before answering.

"Boom, I was overcome by the timing of this little baby being dropped off, last minute with no notice into a family that was already up to their eyeballs in kids who needed so much; you and Kelly. I was overcome by the chance that it would be with all of your best friends in the world present. When things like that happen in our lives, we cannot brush it aside as being mere coincidence. We've all heard about your experiences through fostering kids, but I don't think any of us who hadn't fostered ourselves could comprehend what the power of that Love was all about. The level of commitment, the love, the hope, and the promise you guys bring is incredible. We are able to share your first feelings with this little one. Man, that's a gift that transcends lives, you know? I think everyone here is going to remember the arrival of Cassie as a reminder to all of us how much we mean to one another and how important our year traveling was. I mean, this week has been fabulous before she got here, but now, with Cassie, it seems more like destiny. The people who come into our lives are the ones that shape us into who we become. We are not human without one another." The Unitarian minister looked at me with a smile before adding, "Besides, I think the reason that everybody was so touched and crying about little Cassie is simple. We knew that both you and Kelly knew it was crazy, yet you did it anyways. It's an incredibly selfless act," he said with a smile.

Perhaps Joe was right. Perhaps we were crazy for taking Cassie in. Maybe we were crazy for planning on adopting both her and her sister, Myeisha. Kelly and I had heard this over and over the past ten years, from both friends and family. If true, was this crazy act going to be too much for our family? Had Kelly and I gone too far?

Chapter 12

Doubled over in pain, I struggled to make it to the bathroom adjacent to Kelly's and my bedroom, yet again. This was the seventh time this morning that I had been forced to my knees by the pain that gripped my lower mid section, and it was only 9:30 on this Saturday morning. I had awoken rather early to the pain, and each time, it grew not only worse, but lasted longer as well. Fortunately, Cassie was taking a mid-morning nap, while Myeisha was entertaining herself in the kitchen, coloring with some new crayons she recently received.

The pain had first begun the evening before, as a sharp stinging feeling left me in a cold sweat, unable to move from the bed for several moments. The morning beforehand, Kelly had taken our four children, plus Chiara, to Disney World for the next week, taking our Swiss friend to the Magic Kingdom for her first visit. As the foster children were both too young to appreciate Mickey Mouse, Donald, Goofy, and all the gang, and were also legally unable to travel across state lines without birth parental permission, I had volunteered to stay home with the two. I had hoped to do a little writing on *The Foster Parenting Manual*, a book I had begun earlier in the summer, and, if possible, also do some work in the garden, if Cassie permitted me, that is.

All thoughts of gardening and book writing flew out the window, though, as I lay crippled on the bathroom floor. Though she could not hear me, I moaned in pain, calling for my wife's name. Never before had I felt such pain; it felt like my lower abdomen was going to explode. I knew that I was not pregnant, as science had yet to make that possible, so the promise that I was about to have a baby was out of the question. While I lay there, Cassie began to cry herself, in the crib located in our bedroom. The week-and-a-half-old's cries brought Myeisha into the bathroom to tell me that her sister was awake.

"What wong, Daddy?" she asked in her broken English. Her language skills had improved a great deal the past few months, and she was now beginning to sound like others her age.

"Nothing, Sweetheart," I managed to say, bringing myself to my knees. "Daddy's fine, thank you." I sure didn't feel fine, though. After taking some pain relief medicine, I changed both Myeisha's and Cassie's diapers, and then fed the littlest one a bottle. Up to this point, I had not called Kelly for her diagnosis and remedy as I did not want to disturb her trip. That changed though, when the next wave of pain came, each one growing closer and closer together with time. This last one forced me to place Cassie gently on the floor next to me, as I too fell to my knees once again. Neither one of us was happy with our predicament, as the infant cried out; her tiny lungs issuing the high-pitch squeal that can only come from a tiny baby. Getting back to my feet, I scooped her up, placed her in her crib again, and rushed to the bathroom for my own roller coaster of activity, a little different to the ones Kelly and the kids were enjoying.

A quick call to my wife confirmed my own analysis; I was passing a kidney stone. This was certainly not what I wanted to be doing this weekend. Two small children to take care of, including one who was only days old, and I was spending every other moment hunched over a toilet, trying to deliver my first kidney stone. This was not a landmark moment in my life, and I wished that the stone would quickly depart from my body, feeling like someone had stuck a knife in me, twisting it back and forth. After all, I was on diaper duty, and the children were making sure that they filled their end of the bargain.

The next several hours saw a repetition of the same scene; doubled over in pain, baby crying, and an older one watching me from afar. Fortunately, by 2:30 that afternoon, the clouds of my personal kidney stone thunderstorm parted, and the boulder of a stone passed through my body. The relief I felt was almost instantaneous, as I'm sure it was for the two little ones, as now I could focus on them instead of the large boulder that was lodged within me. As Kelly and I had found the first full week with Cassie, she was going to be another handful, and I would need all my strength to take care of her.

The next week saw me back at work, again between both schools. As it was a week of pre-planning for teachers, the schools would be empty of students, as teachers and school employees were busy preparing for new students, new lessons, and a new school year. The previous Wednesday, when Cassie was one week old, I visited both school principals, explaining to them the situation I was in; a baby, fresh out the womb, an unexpected one at that, and unable to enter into day care of any kind until she was at least six weeks of age, and in our care. As her foster parents, Kelly and I were legally responsible for her care and well-being. As Kelly had planned the trip to Disney months ago, I encouraged her to go, and I would find some way to take care of Cassie. Thus, it was with humble heart and pleas that I approached the principals of both schools, explaining my dilemma. I either had to take the baby to work with me during the week of pre-planning, or I would have to take the week off, due to lack of child care for the baby who was in the custody of DFCS.

Pleading my case, I assured both principals that the baby would stay with me in the media center, as I attended to preparing for the upcoming school year. With no students in the building, it was to be a quiet week anyway. To further my case, I was sure to dress Cassie in a pretty outfit, and placed the baby in the arms of both principals, telling each of the tiny infant's sad history in an attempt at pulling the heartstrings. Fortunately, it worked, and Cassie was able to spend the week with me at work, going from middle school library to high school library. Five years previously, when Grace was only days old and first placed in our home, I took her to work with me as well, during that school's three days of planning. This time, I was an experienced pro, able to juggle a baby bottle and baby in one hand, while working on the computer with the other. Like Gracie before her, Cassie became the darling of both schools, as many teachers found her story heartbreaking and her smile heartwarming. The week with her only helped my love to grow for the helpless foster child, and I was even more devoted to helping her, and to bringing her into my family on a permanent basis.

Like other foster babies before her, Cassie was a victim of her biological parents' abuses and vices, suffering from Neonatal Abstinence Syndrome. Myeisha's mother was taking several drugs while pregnant with Cassie; alcohol, marijuana, and the strong possibility of many more, according to the caseworker. As a result, the first month with Cassie was a challenging one. Though we were certain that she was a blessing to our family, the foster baby presented a difficult time for us as the summer months came to an end, and the beginning of a new school year began. Once again, Kelly and I were faced with a baby who suffered from drugs, the drugs of her mother. As the mother consumed great quantities of drugs during her pregnancy, Cassie had consumed them as well, as the drugs had entered the mother's placenta and into the fetus's tiny body and brain. We were relieved, though, to find that she did not suffer from chlamydia, as it was a false alarm.

Recently, Kelly had conducted a personal study of how marijuana and other drugs affected a baby. What she found not only reinforced what she already knew from her previous study when Grace came to be a part of our family, but she also discovered some new and disturbing information, information that could affect not only Cassie, but Myeisha, too. Drugs, such as marijuana, cocaine, Crack, and alcohol, affect a baby's growth, nervous system, and brain development. Countless studies found that babies exposed to various drugs are at greater risk of attention disorders and learning problems. As my own doctoral study found, many times these learning problems would not show up until a child reached school age, causing a host of problems for the child with academics, along with behavior. Short-term memory and concentration are also at risk for these children. Perhaps what disturbed Kelly the most was that children whose mothers smoked marijuana during pregnancy had a higher risk of leukemia than those mothers who did not. The thought of Cassie and Myeisha facing this greater risk was one that troubled my wife, and sent her into prayer for both of them.

The difficult challenge that lay before us at this moment, though, was the harshness of Cassie's condition in her first month of life. Shortly after we returned from the reunion, the newborn began showing the signs of withdrawal that we had seen in other foster infants. Day and night, the tiny baby screamed as the drugs weaned out of her body, torturing her small frame. Like Grace and the others before her, there was nothing we could do to placate her, to comfort and soothe the suffering child, as the drugs cruelly brought pain and agitation to her. Kelly and I would watch helplessly as Cassie's muscles would tighten up in torment. For the next month, we struggled to feed her, as she refused many times to take a bottle. Sleep was elusive for not only the infant, but for Kelly and me as well. As the crib was in our bedroom, we had a front-row seat to the screams each evening. To be sure, the screams were not only in the nights, but all day as well. We were quickly wearing down, and I began to ask for God's strength to get me through these rough days with the newborn.

By late August, the school year was in full swing. Chiara had returned back home to Switzerland the day before our school year started. Jace began her first year in the school district's marching band, joining Kolby who was a seasoned pro in her third year. Brody was helping out by volunteering to be a manager of sorts, moving equipment and helping others when needed. Grace was beginning her own adventure in school, entering into kindergarten. Watching her own siblings in school, as well as the many foster children who had been living with us and enrolled in our schools as well, the five-year-old was ready to be a part of the education process.

It was during this time when the girls' caseworker, Lisa, mentioned to us that the current boyfriend of the birth mother had expressed an interest in adopting the two. He had traveled to the hospital when Cassie was born, and had mentioned this to the caseworker during that time period, though this was the first we had heard of it. The news of this sent me into combat mode, as I quickly prepared to fight to the finish on this occasion. In the past, I had always fought for all foster children in my home as if they were my own biological children. Yet, there was a different fire burning within me for this fight. It was not simply because we were hoping to adopt these two children, though. Instead, it was because of who the boyfriend was; or to clarify it better, what her boyfriend did for a profession. He was a modern-day pimp.

The fact that an agent of prostitutes was a possible candidate to adopt these two girls was beyond my comprehension. My mind thought of all the potential horrors from this scenario, as the likely reason for adopting these two innocent girls became clear to me. This thought not only disturbed me tremendously, it sent me quickly into action, and I immediately got on the phone and rang the caseworker, preparing myself to take it further. If necessary, I was prepared to take legal action, though the legal rights of a foster parent were slim to none.

Yet there were judges I knew who were sympathetic to my cause, and to the cause of the foster children in my home. I had done just this when Grace's biological mother wanted the then 18-month-old to be adopted by a friend of the family. This friend of the mother's was a young 23-year-old, working two full-time jobs. The danger that I saw at that time was the friend's living conditions; she was living with her 46-year-old boyfriend. My concern lay in the fact, at the time, not that the boyfriend was old enough to be the potential adoptive mother's father, but that both of the boyfriend's own children were in jail, both teens arrested for drugs in the same building, the same school I worked at. I argued with Grace's caseworker that not only could the potential mother not devote her time to the child, working two jobs, but her boyfriend could not commit himself to it either, as he was unable to commit to marrying the 23-year-old. Besides, as I pointed out to the caseworker, I was not too impressed with his own track record of raising children or his parental skills, as both of his sons were in jail. In this case, we were fortunate when the mother's friend decided against pursuing adoption. After a few phone calls by Lisa, we were fortunate, also, when the boyfriend changed his mind this time as well.

Kelly and I had grown quite used to the fact that we would often encounter birth parents in our small, rural town, and had indeed done so many times. Whether it was the public library, a grocery store, gas station, football game, or at the post office, Kelly and I had had both our scheduled and unscheduled visits with birth parents of many of the foster children within our home. In our little village of Monticello, this even became expected, as many knew who we were. After all, the number of foster parents in the entire county was small, and the number of Australians was even smaller, with the exact number totaling one. Unless, of course, Brody, Jace, and Kolby were included, as all three held an Australian passport, the three having dual citizenship of both nations due to their birthright.

Therefore, my surprise was all the greater when I encountered some birth family members of Cassie and Myeisha at a high school football game in a nearby town one Friday evening. As Kolby and Jace were now playing in the school's marching band, and Brody was the manager, Kelly and I were now taking part in traveling to the away games. On this particular fall evening, we had taken the two foster children with us, along with Grace, and had driven the hour-long ride. The autumn air was crisp, and the smell of burning leaves throughout the small town wafted through the bleachers.

A mixture of brown, orange, and yellow leaves circled in the sky, as the light breeze pushed the decaying foliage across the football field. Like Monticello, the town folk turned out to support their high school students, and the bleachers on the home side were full. At half time, Kelly and I took the three little ones to the opposite side of the field, joining the home-side residents as it offered a better vantage point to view both marching bands. As Kolby had been marching for three years now, we had become experts in all things marching musically.

I had become used to the sideway glances, heads turning, and stares from others when out with Grace. Her dark skin color was significantly darker than my own peach-flavored skin tone, leading many to question why she was with me. This, of course, led to many jokes on my behalf, with me even informing one inquisitive person that Grace was not African American, but Australian American, as her mother, albeit an adoptive one, hailed from the Land Down Under.

Taking Myeisha by the hand, I cradled Cassie in the free arm, while Kelly walked behind me, holding onto Grace's hand. The bleachers were emptying themselves, as people raced to restrooms, concession stands, and others simply to stretch their legs. Kelly and I struggled mightily to make our way up the stairs of the opposing side's bleachers. As I was half way up the metal stairs, I felt a light patting on my shoulder. Turning around, I found a large, heavy set lady looking Kelly and me up and down. A baffled look was firmly planted upon the middle-aged woman's face, as she smiled in a perplexed fashion.

"Those cheeldern sure are purty lookin. Are dey yur kids?" she asked, noticeably bewildered. Kelly and I were a confusing picture to those that did not know us; two "white" adults with three "black" children. My wife and I had long ago done away with those two divisive terms, "black" and "white" people, and did not allow our children to paint others in the racially tainted way of identification.

Forcing a smile from my face that was ready to burst forth, I looked at her in a straight face. "Yes, ma'am, they are ours." I then paused for what was only one second, allowing time for the all-so-important pregnant pause, before continuing on. "We just have really recessive genes," I then added, and was met with a most confused look. Smiling politely at her, I continued on up the stairs, while Kelly tried to explain that her husband was not only just joking, but that he was slightly nuts.

After the halftime show had ended, Kelly and I rushed down to the field to congratulate not only our own children, but the entire squad for a job well done. From there, we returned back to the visitor side for the second half of the show. Kelly took Grace to the restroom, while I continued on my way. As I neared the bleachers, I was stopped by someone calling my name.

"Hello. How are you?" I smiled, though I was not familiar with the face. I was used to this in Monticello, where everyone knew me as "the guy who married Kelly." This time, I was a little startled, as we were in a town I had only passed through years ago in my professional wrestling days.

"I'm great!" she replied, with a friendly smile. "Is that Myeisha and her sister?" she asked, pointing to the two foster girls.

"Yes, ma'am, it is," I answered, choosing to use the polite Southern response that is so common in Georgia.

Pointing to Cassie, she responded as so many others had the past month. "She's so pretty. I haven't had a chance to see her yet. What's her name?"

Did I hear correctly? She had not had a chance to meet Cassie yet? Who was this person? My mind was racing for possible answers, though none were coming to me. I felt my heartbeat quicken as I answered, "Well, we're not quite sure how to pronounce her first name, so we are just calling her Cassie."

"That's a nice name. Can I hold her?"

"Sure," I said, holding the three-month-old over to her.

"Thanks; she's beautiful," she said smiling in return, before hitting me with an unexpected claim. "You know, I'm the one who thought about adopting her." The words sent tremors through my body, as I was completely unprepared for this encounter. Here was the aunt that we were told about earlier this year, right before we went to Australia. Here was the family member that Lisa had informed us about that was trying to adopt Myeisha. Kelly and I were so shaken originally by this news that we had entered a brief time of grief and despair, deeply saddened by the possibility that we would lose Myeisha. Hurry up, Kelly, I thought to myself. I needed her reassuring voice and warm smile right now.

What was I to say to this? I felt awkward, unsure how to respond. Yet, I had to say something, and quickly. "Oh, it's nice to meet you," I managed to get out. After saying it, I quickly began to pray silently to myself, asking God to give me wisdom in the words I next spoke, and understanding for the moment. Suddenly, I recognized her as someone who had worked at the high school as a substitute teacher from time to time. She had always seemed friendly, cordial, and quite polite.

"Yes, I had thought seriously about adopting Myeisha. I'm her daddy's aunt, and I wanted to keep her in the family. I prayed and prayed about it, and was planning on adopting her, but then I found out that the mother was pregnant again. Dr. DeGarmo, I just don't think I can take a baby in right now," she said, with not only a smile on her face, but I could hear the smile in her inflection, as well. As I had grappled with the same decision, I completely understood her concerns. I wasn't so sure I could handle it myself.

"I understand, ma'am, and I can assure you that she is in a good home," I said.

"I know she is, and that's why I struggled with this. I know you and your wife are good people, and that Myeisha is loved. But when I heard there was going to be another baby, well, it felt like God had answered my prayers, telling me to let it go. Dr. DeGarmo, I felt like He was telling me that Myeisha and that baby were just where they were supposed to be, with you and your wife."

Her words put me at ease, and I felt the tension in my shoulders begin to relax, the stress of the situation beginning to slip away. By this point, Kelly had approached, and Myeisha ran up to her, embracing her mother of 16 months. Thanking her for the kind words, I introduced her to Kelly. "Hey, Kel, this is Myeisha's aunt," I said, giving my wife a sudden and quick introduction. She hid her own surprise well, and the two chatted for a few minutes. The aunt asked if Myeisha and Cassie could come over and visit with the family some time, and Kelly happily obliged the request. As the second half of the game had started, we politely excused ourselves and headed back to the bleachers. It seemed that the reach of our foster and adoptive children was extending out further into our lives, leaving us no avenue to escape from the world of biological family.

With the possible and planned adoption of two more, our house suddenly seemed smaller. Indeed, we had harbored seven children before on several occasions, but those were only temporary situations as foster parents. Cassie and Myeisha's permanent addition in the house meant permanent living conditions needed to be made.

A year ago, we had converted a storage room in our basement into another bedroom, one that our foster children and guests used when needed. This added bedroom brought the total to six in our home, as Brody, Jace, Grace, and Kolby all had their own, along with Kelly and mine, of course. The addition of the two little ones as full-time members of the DeGarmo stable posed a problem; where would they sleep? There were several possibilities before us. First, as Kolby was now in tenth grade in high school, she only had three more years of school left before moving out and moving on to college. The girls could take her room at that time. Second, Jace had the largest room in the house, an attic space that was converted into a bedroom long ago. At one time, Brody and Sydney both shared that room, and it could be converted again into a two-person bedroom, if needed. There was also the guest room, which could be converted into a full-time room for children as well.

None of these possibilities appealed to my wife, as she did not want to move a child from their room, or give up the privacy that each had enjoyed for so long. The idea of turning the guest room into a child's room was one that did not appeal to me either. Living so far from Kelly's side of the family resulted in guests from Australia staying a long time, and a guest room was needed for these occasions. Thus, it was time to think outside the box, so to speak, leading us to think outside our house. An addition to the house might be the answer. Kelly and I began looking at plans to take the hot tub out, under a section of our upper deck porch, and instead convert that area into a bedroom, extending the basement living area. This added bedroom, if built, would be used for both Cassie and Myeisha, and would give Brody some additional family members in the basement with him each evening.

For the past few months, I had been speaking at foster parent associations throughout the state, as well as throughout the nation, in the capacity as a trainer. Along with this, I was speaking at churches, libraries, and other organizations about foster care. With my doctoral studies behind me, I had been in prayer about what I might do with the degree. Writing for various foster parent magazines, both in the United States and in Europe, was one area I had also recently begun, and as I enjoyed the writing process with my doctorate, this was a simple transition. Speaking also came quite easily to me, perhaps due to my years as a high school classroom teacher, and my many years as a performer and entertainer. I truly enjoyed speaking and training foster parents, as I was able to meet those who helped children in need from all corners of the nation.

It was at one such training session that I was met with a surprise: a reunion with two of our former foster children. One of the questions that I was frequently asked by those outside of the foster care system was how many former foster children were Kelly and I in contact with. Sadly, the number was only one, Helena, outside of Grace, of course. The past decade had seen over 30 children come through our home, 30 children whom we had come to love, nourish, care for, and provide for. Yet Helena was the only one we had contact with. Despite attempts at reaching out to some, including our Sydney, we were met with poor results. Kelly and I had found that there were those birth parents that considered foster parents the "bad guys," so to speak, and did not wish their own children to communicate with or have any relationship with their former foster parents. Whatever their reasoning might be, there were many relationships in our lives that were left unresolved, and Kelly and I spent time in prayer for these children, hoping that they were okay, that they were safe, and that they were loved. After all, each time a child left our home, we were losing a member of our family, and this can be traumatic too.

According to Kubler-Ross's well-known stages of grief there are several stages a foster parent may experience when a foster child leaves the home. These include shock, denial, anger, guilt, bargaining, depression, and then finally acceptance. Indeed, I went through many of these feelings myself, through the years, and have still not completely embraced the fact that some children have moved on. I often tell people that fostering is the hardest job one can do. One of the reasons why is that fostering is not only hard work, it is also heart work. Good foster parents place their entire heart into taking care of these children in need, children that were often much more difficult to parent and more demanding of time, and we had surely done that through the years.

"Excuse me, John," I heard a voice behind me say, "I have some kids here that you might want to see." I was talking with one of the caseworkers at the county's child welfare office, and excused myself to turn around. As I was in a nearby county to the one Kelly and I lived in, I was not surprised to find Laurie smiling at me, a foster parent whom Kelly and I had worked with in the past. Years ago, when Scotty lived with us, he had moved from our home to Laurie and her husband Mike, as the young four-year-old boy was readying for adoption with another family. While Laurie and Mike did not adopt Scotty, they were in the final stages of adopting two other foster children.

"Hey Laurie, it's great to see you," I said. Not recognizing the two children next to her, I smiled at them.

"John, this is Espn and Melinda, and we are about to adopt them."

At once, a smile broke upon my face. "Oh my goodness! Hello, how are you?" I said, with laughter from the joy I suddenly felt after seeing the two after so many years. How many years had it been? Was it four? I wasn't sure myself. The two children looked great. Melinda was only a baby when I last saw her, one that suffered terribly from her own withdrawal problems, and here she was, a healthy little girl, not much younger looking than our own Gracie. Espn looked even better, and I shook his hand as Laurie filled me in on their plans to not only adopt the two, but to change their names as well, much like we had done with Grace, and were planning on with Myeisha and her sister.

After the training seminar ended, I drove home, anxious to tell Kelly about my encounter with our two former foster children. It was wonderful to see them after all these years, and even better to see them in a loving and stable home. That night, we lifted up Laurie and Mike in praying, thanking God for their gift of a home to these two children, and asking Him to bless the family with His love and grace. Laurie and Mike had made a difference in the lives of these children, a tremendous difference. Yet, what about Micah; what about Scotty; what about Logan; and what about Sydney? There were so many children in need, and so many had left our own home to face an uncertain and even frightening future. Were Kelly and I doing all we could? Were we making a difference? As I tried to sleep that night, I was met with the thought that I could have done more for the children who left my home. I could have done more.

Chapter 13

The church hall was a crowded one, with children running between tables, while the parents watched with smiles upon their faces. We were at our foster parent association's annual Christmas party, held at a local church, where the county's foster parents came together each year at this time in order to give our foster children a special Christmas. I had discovered years ago that sadly many foster children have never truly celebrated a Christmas or birthday before coming into care. To be sure, Kelly and I had been witness to a few children not know how to open a wrapped present before coming to our home. Our association, like so many others across the country, tried to make the holiday an extra special one; one where the children could forget about the abuse, the pain, and the sadness they so keenly felt on a daily basis. Santa Claus had just given each of the children some wrapped presents, and was now hosting me in his lap. As I did every year, I asked him for a national championship for my beloved Michigan State's basketball squad. Wishing him a merry Christmas, I eased off his lap, listening to the giggles of the other children who were watching me from nearby. "Daddy, you can't get on Santa's lap," Brailey told me. We had reverted to calling her full time, now, by what we hoped was her adoptive name.

"Why not, little one?" I said, a hearty laugh breaking forth from me. I had been sitting in Santa's lap each year for as long back as I could remember. In fact, when Kelly first came to the United States the year after we traveled in Up With People, it was around late Christmas time, and I had convinced her to get our picture together on top of Santa's lap. Little did she know at that time that we would be married 20 years later, and I would still be sitting on his lap.

"Daddy," Brailey said, laughing along with me, "you're too heavy."

"Oh, I think it will be okay, Sweetheart," I replied, bending to give her a kiss on her forehead. The three-year-old had celebrated her birthday just the week before, and had been with us for a year and a half now. We were still waiting on the final clearance for the adoption of both her and her now six-month-old sister to go through, and I was a little apprehensive that something still might block it from happening. As she ran off to join the others, I walked over to Chris and Paula, who were each holding a small child in their arms. We had been interrupted earlier in our conversation, as the foster couple had begun to tell me about the two new children placed in their home.

The two had already adopted a child from care, and were two of the loveliest people I had come across; so gentle and caring in their love for children. The story they told me about their two new ones was a heartbreaking one, and one that I had a difficult time coming to grips with. The tiny 18-month-old, who was placed in their home three months ago, was legally blind, due simply to the negligence of her biological mother. Little Angela's brown eyes were abnormally large, due to her blindness, a condition that was completely preventable. The young foster girl's mother, who stayed home with the infant due to her unemployment, was to only place a drop of medicine in her daughter's eyes each day; only a drop each. Yet, she had not, and I was told that the young teenaged mother instead sat and watched television all day long. As a result, this tiny child was now blind for life.

As disturbing as this was, Chris and Paula's second child's story was even more traumatic. Just a few days earlier, the foster couple had taken in a six-month-old boy into their home. This second foster child of theirs had suffered terribly. When Chris related to me that the boyfriend of the baby's mother had dipped the infant in boiling hot water as a form of punishment, I was stunned into silence, as there were no words for this horror. Even more distressing was the fact that the mother did not take the child to the hospital right away, but waited 24 hours, leaving the infant in his crib, his flesh burning off his legs. Several skin grafts later, Chris told me that the doctors believe the child will never walk.

"And John, what's really worrying is that the mother is still with the boyfriend. She won't even leave him, even though he did this to her baby." The look on the foster parent's face was one of pain and grief, as he held the infant in his arms. Both of the small foster baby's legs were encased in casts, reaching up to the infant's waist. My heart ached for both the children, as well as for Chris and Paula, who had their hands full with the two little ones. Later that evening, I took some time to reflect upon the suffering of both of the children, both so very young. During this Christmas season of joy, when we celebrate the birth of a baby, I could not understand how two other little babies had been so traumatized. To be sure, this was a season of forgiveness, even for those who had caused so much pain for these children. Yet, why should these children have to experience such horrors? Why did they have to be born into a world of anguish and torture?

* * *

After placing the groceries on the kitchen counter, I signaled for Kelly to come follow me into the bedroom. Closing the door behind her, I placed the gift bag into her arms. "Open it," I said, with urgency in my voice.

"I'll do it later," she said. "I have to go and make lunch for the kids, and feed the baby."

"Kolby and Jace can watch the little ones for a minute," I answered. "This will just take a second. I really think you need to have a look at what's in there."

Opening the gift bag, decorated with Christmas images, she took out a box. "What is it?" she asked, looking at me. Smiling at her, I motioned for her to open up the box. "Oh my gosh, is it…?" Her question was only half out of her mouth before she stopped, a slight gasp escaping her Australian lips. "This isn't what I think it is, is it?" she continued, a hint of a smile in her eyes.

"It's a Nook," I smiled back at her. In truth, it was more than a smile, as I was beaming. "They're like Kindles; you know, those eBook readers everyone seems to be talking about. There are actually five of them in there," I said, pointing to the bag with my right hand, as the left came to sit upon my wife's shoulder. "Bill and Beth, from church, gave them to us."

Confusion coming over Kelly's face, she asked, "I don't understand. What do you mean they gave them to us?"

Taking the bag out of her arms, I took her hands in mine, standing next to the bed. "Well, I was in the choir room, putting my choir robe on. I was in a hurry, as I was late to the little practice we have before the service. Bill and Beth came into the choir room, and I told them that it was great to see them, as I hadn't seen them in a while. We spoke for just a moment, and then she handed the bag to me. When I opened it up and saw the Nooks, I didn't know what to say. Honestly, Kelly, their generosity left me speechless. She told me that the Nooks were for each of the children living in our homes, and that they appreciated what we do for foster children."

"What did you say then?" my wife asked.

"Nothing! I just didn't know what to say." Shrugging my shoulders, I continued, "Instead, I just gave them a big hug each, and tried to wipe the tears that were starting. Kelly, this is just…incredible. I mean, Bill and Beth did not have to do this. These weren't cheap, you know. It's just amazing."

"Yes, God is so good to us. Let's take a second and pray," Kelly said, while closing her eyes. "Dear Lord, thank You for this blessing. Thank You for our church family, and for people like Bill and Beth. Jesus, we are grateful for what You do for us, and thank You for this gift. Please bless these two with Your love, as well. Amen."

Giving me a quick hug, she turned to walk into the kitchen, and return to a kitchen full of hungry children, with me following her a few moments later, after a quick change of clothes. I was still thinking about the Nooks an hour later when I drove off to the Atlanta airport to pick up Kelly's mother, Shirley, and her aunt, Trish. The two Aussies were coming to our home for the next four weeks, to celebrate the Christmas holidays with us. It was a few hours later when I returned with the two, exhausted from their long equator-crossing trip. Nevertheless, they were happy to see Kelly and the children. The next few days saw Trish fall in love with Cassie. As they had often done in the past, Shirley and Trish found a need in our home, and filled it. Two days after they arrived, we had the gift of a brand new, industrial-sized wash machine. Despite my pleas for them to spend their money elsewhere, the two Aussies felt we needed a bigger wash machine, and wanted to help us, as we helped the children.

For quite some time, Kelly had shared with me the guilt she would feel when people donated gifts to us. Our church family, and our Up With People family, would often send us clothes, bake us meals, or help out in other ways. Indeed, just weeks before, Dave from Up With People sent us a large box of clothing for Cassie. Along with that, Lynne and Steve once again wanted to help out by purchasing gifts for the foster children in our home. I tried to reassure my own Aussie, Kelly, that this was one way people felt they could help foster children.

"Not everyone feels they can be foster parents," I told her, after we had received the gift from Dave. "This is a way, though, that people, like Dave and others, can help foster children. By helping us, they are helping children in care."

"But it's too much," she replied. "We just can't keep letting people give us clothes and food, and even money. I feel guilty about it."

"I know, but, Kelly, people want to help us. This is their way of serving God, and of helping children. These gifts may be the only way they can help foster children. Let them do it, Kelly. They want to help out," I tried to reassure her.

Now, a month later, it was Kelly's turn to convince me that we should take the gift of a wash machine. After all, we did have a house full of children, and our regular wash machine was running nonstop each day, trying to catch up. I was most grateful for the gift, and soon came to realize that an industrial wash machine was just what we needed. Cassie, Brailey, Grace, Brody, Jace, and Kolby were going through clothes like no one's business each day. Jace and Kolby had discovered the fine art of fashion, and felt the necessity of wearing the latest fashions and clothing designs every time they stepped outside their bedroom doors. Brody and Grace went through clothing just as quick, though for a different reason; these two were outside all day long, and needed fresh changes of clothing throughout each day, as they both seemed to find each and every pile of dirt, mud, and grime that existed in our six acres of land. Brailey has also felt the call of fashion, in her own way, and would change at least 12 times a day, if allowed. The oldest foster child in our home fancied herself a princess, and had amassed a number of frilly dresses and plastic high heel shoes. Of course, like any good princess, she had to show off the fine clothing to her court; our family. Finally, Cassie was just six months old, and was the typical baby in regards to getting herself dirty and wet, too. The new wash machine was maybe just about the best gift we had received since the homemade ice-cream maker our children and I so deeply treasured.

Yet disaster struck just a week later. It was four days before Christmas, and all through the house, there were ten people who were going through clothes, sheets, and towels at a rapid pace, and with an eleventh person soon to arrive, with many a blouse. Helena was coming to spend a day or two over Christmas with us. The new wash machine was more important than ever. With so many people in our home, the industrial-sized marvel was running three times a day, at a minimum. It rapidly became a staple of our home; a much-needed and depended-upon member of our family; an icon amongst the DeGarmo appliances.

"Kelly, did you notice that the wash machine door won't close?" My question rang out from our pantry, as I was loading in yet another pile of wet towels.

"What's wrong with it?" she replied back, with a question of her own.

"Not sure," I said, with a tinge of concern in my voice. "The door just won't close properly. I can't seem to get it to shut."

Joining me in the pantry a moment later, she tried her luck with it, but met the same fate that I did. After a brief discussion, in which we both agreed that our Wonder Wash Machine was not performing so wonderfully for us, I placed a call to the store where it was purchased. I was quick to point out to the individual on the other end of the phone that the machine was brand new, and still under warranty.

"Yeah, there have been reports of this problem all over the country," the store employee informed me. "Some defect with the lock on the door. We can have someone come to yur house and repair it for ya."

A sense of relief immediately washed over me, as I could see that this crisis of dirty clothes doom was to be averted. "When might I expect you?" I asked, believing that it would be in the next day or so.

"Oh, we have a lot of these to get to. It will be in the next ten days to two weeks."

"Ten days to two weeks?" I blurted out. This was madness! I had far too many people in the house which needed the affectionate caress of the Wonder Wash. Trying to remain calm, I tried to appeal to his Christmas spirit. "I have 11 people in my house, and if I don't get a wash machine working any time soon, I am going to be under a mountain of clothing. I need a Christmas miracle!" This last sentence was implored with heightened emotion, as visions of a dirty clothes avalanche stormed through my head.

I heard him laugh over the phone. At least my plea of desperation entertained him, I thought to myself. "Okay, I'll see what I kin do for ya," he replied. "I'll try to get it fixed fer ya right after Christmas."

"That would be great!" I exclaimed, exhaling in a sigh of relief. It was amazing how we had come to depend on the appliance so much. With the Christmas two-week holiday, I knew that we would depend on it even more so, as everyone would be home from both school and work.

Four days later, it was Christmas morning, and it was another magical Christmas day at our house. Presents were piled under the tree that morning, as Santa Claus once again managed to make his way down our chimney. Helena spent the day with us, which made it all the more special, making the number 11 in the household that day. The former foster daughter of ours had truly become a valued and loved member of our family, and Kelly and I considered her another daughter of ours. After enduring so much pain, suffering and betrayal growing up, the Romanian-born girl had turned into a wonderful young lady. Holding Cassie much of the morning, she regaled us with many stories of her experiences in college. It was a special day; it was a noisy day. Peals of laughter and joy rang through the house, alongside the Christmas music, and the din of the occasional whining baby. The noise at times would rise to a very loud decibel and I would not have had it any way else.

* * *

"Why is Michael screaming like that?" Kelly asked, as I climbed to the top basement stairs into the kitchen.

"He said he doesn't want to go to bed," I replied, with weariness. It had been a long February night with this newest child from foster care. Ten-year-old Michael had arrived at our house earlier that afternoon. Along with his two younger brothers, Michael had been placed into Jason and Tammy's home two months earlier. Like most foster parents, Jason and Tammy had not had a vacation in years, as they had been caring for children without much of a break for quite some time now. Feeling the need to spend time with just their own girls, all three adopted from foster care, they had embarked on a week-long cruise. Both Kelly and I were excited for them, as they deserved a break, and we were happy to help out by taking Michael into our family for the week. As our house was already full with six other children, we felt we were only able to take care of one additional child, as nine seemed simply too overwhelming, and even impossible. As a result, Michael's two younger siblings were placed in another home in a nearby county for the week, and our house once again returned to seven children.

Seven children! Michael almost seemed like seven by himself. Tammy had given us prior warning a few days beforehand about Michael's behavior. Though she would not go into detail, she did inform us that the young ten-year-old had suffered from some of the most horrific abuse that she had ever come to know; abuse that had traumatically affected him in a number of ways, including violent outbursts. We were witness to one of those outbursts of violence at that very moment, as the child continued his screaming assault upon our ears.

"The poor boy," my wife said, compassion very evident in her voice. Her eyes also betrayed her emotions, as the sadness she felt for Michael reflected easily for me to see. "He's simply afraid, and doesn't understand why he's here."

"Yeah, you're right," I agreed, "but he's been screaming now for about an hour. He's got some strong lungs." I smiled, trying to lighten the mood a little. I had spent the past 45 minutes trying several different strategies in an attempt at comforting the young boy. When Jason and Tammy dropped him off, the foster parents reassured him of their love for him, giving him a hug and kiss before they left. I suspected a little trouble ahead when I noted that the child gave no indication that he heard them, nor returned any of their love, as he went straight towards the plate of chocolate chip cookies. When bedtime arrived hours later, I tucked Michael into bed with as much warmth and comfort as possible. The ten-year-old refused to stay under the blankets, springing up from the bed, yelling that he did not want to go to sleep, and that he didn't want to be in our house. "I don't want to be here," he yelled, his face red with anger. "I want to go home!"

"I understand, Michael, and you will go home with Miss Tammy and Mr. Jason in a few days. They just…"

"I don't want to go to their house," he interrupted, the volume of his voice rising in decibels. "I hate it there! I want to go home!"

"I know you want to go home, son, and…"

"I want to go home!" he interrupted once again, this time even louder, punctuating each word with an intensity that was disturbing. By this time, he was lying flat on his back, his feet towards the pillow, and his arms flaying in anger.

Trying a different tactic, I attempted to ease Michael's anxieties by offering to read him a book. "Son, would you like me to read you a story?"

"I want to go home!" he screamed back.

"I know, son. Tell you what; I'm going to leave a few books here, and you can look at the books for a while if you like."

"I don't want to," he replied loudly. For the next several moments, I tried to calm the frightened and anxiety-filled young child, to no avail. Michael only grew more enraged at each passing attempt. During my doctoral studies, I grew to learn about Reactive Attachment Disorder (RAD), a condition in which children have great difficulty in forming healthy attachments with others. Along with this, these children also struggle mightily with connecting with others on any type of social level. Children who are diagnosed with RAD also find it very difficult to keep their emotions in control. As a child with RAD grows older, his symptoms may grow more troublesome and difficult to manage. Anger issues may begin to develop, as the child might lash out in tantrums and/or uncontrolled rage, or act in a passive aggressive manner.

While most with RAD will endeavor to remain in control in an attempt to avoid a feeling of helplessness, many times, these children will instead act defiant and disobedient, and will be quick to argue with another. Others with the same disorder may withdraw from others, like they had in infancy. These children will seek to avoid interaction with others, including their peers, and act in an awkward and uncomfortable fashion while around others. Some children will strive to distance themselves from any type of physical contact with another, as they may perceive this interaction as a threat of some sort. Furthermore, these children will be more likely to seek out an affectionate relationship that is inappropriate with another, even those they do not know, yet display little or no affection towards their parents or caretakers. Was Michael suffering from this disorder? His anger and rage seemed to indicate that he might indeed suffer from it. The young foster child was on medication for his disorder, and, while Kelly and I were of the belief that many children in foster care were overmedicated, Michael seemed to be in need of something, at least.

We took Jason and Tammy's advice the next day, and borrowed some of Brody's Legos. The foster couple had discovered that Michael loved the colorful interlocking toys, and would spend hours lost in a world of building. As it was a Saturday, Kelly was at work, and I was on child care. After lunch, I put both Cassie and Brailey down for a nap, and put on a Disney movie for Grace. The older children were all working on school work or reading and I sat down at the kitchen table to do some writing. With a bucket load of Brody's Legos on the floor next to him, Michael became completely engaged in construction. Strangely, the boy who spent the past two nights full of rage was now as silent and as calm as a still summer day. When Kelly arrived home later that afternoon, the young ten-year-old ran to her and gave her a hug. Indeed, the troubled child felt very comfortable around her, and had given my wife many hugs since he arrived.

Dinner time, though, was a different chapter in this story that night. All throughout the meal, Michael was fidgeting in his chair, and would complain about the food. When it came time for dessert, our newest family member indicated that he was not so fond of the way it was prepared for him. Kelly had made him a banana split, with some of our homemade ice cream. As she placed the bowl in front of him, Michael exploded in fury.

"This isn't cut right!" the child blasted.

"What's wrong with it, Honey?" Kelly asked, not flinching an inch from this sudden storm of wrath. After all, we had weathered many a foster frenzy during the years, and had both become seasoned veterans. "I thought you like bananas," she said, placing her arm on his shoulder in an attempt to comfort him.

Her gesture did little to bring tranquility to the moment, as Michael's anger only seemed to increase. "They're long ways! They're supposed to be cut in half!" he yelled, shoving the bowl away from him in his right hand, while pounding the table with his left.

Without saying a word, I walked over to the table, picked up the bowl, and placed it in the freezer a few seconds later. With this, the distressed child gripped the table and began to shake it violently, screaming at a level that our neighbors surely heard four houses away. "Michael, we don't act that way in our house," Kelly said. "I'm afraid that dinner time is over for you, and there will not be any dessert tonight. We can try tomorrow night, though, okay?"

This apparently was not okay for him, as Michael continued to shake the table, screaming all the louder, if it was humanly possible. With this, dinner was over for everyone else, as the other children quickly deserted their chairs, not wishing to listen to Michael's assault on our ear drums, and our meal.

The pattern was much the same that week; harmony with Legos, and anger over small issues. Michael did like being around Brody, and often wanted to play with him, with our son obliging him, sitting down on the lounge room floor next to the ten-year-old and constructing Lego cars and other creations with him. Yet, when it came time for bedtime each evening, the screaming and kicking began once again. By the time the week was over, we were ready for Jason and Tammy to pick up Michael. It had been an exhausting week, both physically and emotionally. The seven days with Michael had seemed like seven weeks, or more. With Michael's departure, we were back down to six children, and the house seemed quiet.

"That's it, Boomie; I'm done fostering. I can't do it any more," my wife said that evening, when the two of us finally made our way to bed. "I'm tired and my migraines aren't going away. Besides, I think it's time we just focus on our own children."

Nodding my head, I didn't try to argue with her. I was becoming worried about Kelly's health, as her migraines were only increasing. What's more, she had been saying the same thing for a number of years now. Maybe God was telling us that our time as foster parents was coming to an end.

Chapter 14

"**B**oom, that's Cathy on the phone about some children. Just pray about it, and do what's best," my wife shouted down to me. It was 5:30 on a Monday evening, and I was just about to light a fire in the pot-belly stove in the basement library, while Kelly was upstairs getting dinner ready.

"What?" I answered back, loud enough for my voice to carry upstairs. Michael had only been gone from the house for eight days, and I distinctly recalled Kelly saying that she was well and truly finished with foster parenting. "I thought you said…"

Before I could finish my sentence, she interrupted me. "Yes, I know. Just pray about it, and do what you think is best. I already talked to her."

The conversation only took a few seconds, and I was able to answer the phone before the answering machine kicked on. "Hello," I said, steeling myself for what might be coming. Even after 11 years of taking these types of calls, I still felt a wave of anxiety sweep through me. How many children this time? How old are they? Why are they coming into care? How long might they need to stay with us? How severe might the abuse be? These were questions that always rushed to the forefront of my mind when taking the Call from DFCS. This time was no different.

"Hey, John, it's Cathy. How are you?" the caseworker asked, with the usual gentleness evident in her voice.

"Hi, Cathy. I'm good, thanks. Kelly just told me that you already spoke with her. What can we do for you?"

"Well, John, I want to know if you can take a child in tonight. It's an emergency situation."

"How old is the child?" I asked; a standard question of mine when trying to find out information about the possible new family members of ours. Kelly and I had a general rule that the children coming to our home were not to be any older than Kolby. We did make exceptions to that rule in the past, though.

"He's 13 years old, and there are four other siblings. You might know him, as the family is from Monticello," she replied, arousing my curiosity. As I worked in the school system, there was a good chance that I might indeed know him. Continuing, she said, "His name is Stephen Mall."

Recognizing the name immediately, I hesitated before answering. "Cathy, he's the worst student in school. His behavior problems are off the charts. I think he also may be in Jace's class. I'll have to talk about this with Kelly, and pray about it. Can I call you back in a few minutes?" Cathy agreed to my request and thanked me before hanging up. By that point, Kelly had come downstairs, and was standing next to me. I was still on my knees, trying to get the fire started, as the temperature was rapidly dropping outside. It promised to be a cold night.

"Well?" she said, looking at me for an answer.

After lighting the match, and setting fire to the balled-up newspaper and sticks in the stove, I closed the door of the pot belly, looking up at my wife afterwards. "Kelly, I'm not sure. He's the worst behaved student in school. I know him by both reputation, and have seen him in action. He's in Jace's grade, you know."

"Yeah, I know. Cathy told me his name, too. I asked Jace if she would be okay with him coming to stay with us. Jace told me that he was in her class before being placed into Alternative School, and that he's fine."

"Well, I thought you wanted to be done," I reminded her.

"I know," she sighed, with a look of resignation, "but this is someone in Jace's class, and he's afraid right now; probably scared. He needs to be with people he knows, and he knows you. Maybe we should." Once again, I was amazed at my wife's ability to love any and all children, and to take care of those who were in need of help, placing these children before her own needs and concerns. She was clearly tired, as the past 11 years had been completely exhausting and draining, yet here she was, once again, ready to take in a child into her home, and into her heart. After a quick prayer, we both agreed to take him in, and I called Cathy back.

"That's great, John, I really appreciate what you and Kelly do. Now, if you will take one child, will you take two?" she asked.

"Hmm," I said, briefly pausing to reflect. "Okay, we can do it."

"Great!" the caseworker replied with enthusiasm. Her next question was almost humorous, if not for the seriousness of the situation. "Well, if you will take two, will you take three?"

"No more than three!" I shot back, with a nervous laugh. "That's all, Cathy, or you will have to give me not only the foster mobile, but the foster hotel, too."

"Okay, thanks, John. Timmy is age nine, and Alicia is ten. The other two will go to Patsy and Mike's house. I really appreciate it. The caseworker will be over in about an hour with the children."

"Great. Kelly and I will be going to the movies tonight, so please tell the caseworker just to drop them off, and we will be home by ten." I enjoyed joking with Cathy, as she was always a good sport. The reality was that Kelly and I had not had a date in quite some time, due to the many foster children in and out of our home.

"What?" the caseworker responded, in a loud voice.

"Just joking, Cathy," I said, laughing aloud. "We'll be here waiting."

"Don't do that to me, John," Cathy said, with relief in her voice. "Tell Kelly I said thanks. You two are so wonderful."

The conversation over, I checked the fire to make sure it was going, and walked upstairs to share the news with Kelly. Nine children; I was going to have nine children sleeping in my house that night, and nine children to get ready in the morning. I had now gone dangerously past the Brady Bunch level, and still no Alice to help us. What was I doing? When I told Kelly about the addition of two more, she smiled, and lifted up a prayer for the two of us, as well as the three children.

Calling the children into the kitchen, we informed them of their newest siblings. "Are they brown?" Grace asked. "Then we would be a whole brown family."

"I don't think so, Sweetheart," Kelly said, giving the child a kiss on the cheek. Brailey danced around the kitchen, excited about the upcoming arrival of more children into the house, while Kolby and Jace left the kitchen to prepare for gymnastic lessons. Hope, a friend of ours and mother of Jace's dear friend Sinclair, was moments away from picking up the two, driving them to a nearby city for their weekly lessons. There was a great deal going on already; adding three more children just added to the normal business that our family underwent every night.

An hour later saw us sitting across from Belinda, the caseworker assigned to the case and now to the county. Timmy, Alicia, and Stephen were downstairs, watching television with Kolby, Jace, and Brody. When the three first arrived, 15 minutes prior, they appeared oddly happy to be with us, and Stephen thanked us for taking him and his two siblings into our home. Normally, children are often quite scared when arriving at a foster parent's house, as it is a very traumatic experience. Being removed suddenly from one's home, one's parents, and one's family and being placed in a strange home with strange people, with often no explanation, is a frightening experience for most foster children. Kelly and I had become rather accustomed to welcoming scared and crying children into our homes. This time, though, was different. As all three were very hungry, we quickly made some sandwiches for them. It appeared as if they had not eaten for some time, as they wolfed down the food before them.

"This was the most disturbing removal I have ever been a part of," Belinda told Kelly and me, as we began signing the necessary paperwork. "I worked in Atlanta for years, and never saw anything like this. It was horrible."

"What do you mean?" my wife asked, sipping on her cappuccino while holding Cassie at the same time.

"It was…awful," she shuddered. "First of all, there was no electricity, no plumbing, no running water, no heat, and no food in the house. There were also large holes in the bedrooms, covered over with blue plastic tarp. But what's worse is that I can honestly tell you that you couldn't see any of the floor in the entire house, as there was so much feces covering the floor." Belinda's face easily expressed the horror she both saw and felt.

"Feces? Human feces?" I whispered aloud, half to myself, taken aback by this revelation.

"I think there was a lot of that, mixed in with dog feces. One of the sheriff deputies who went into the house to retrieve the children had to walk back out of the house, as he was getting sick to his stomach from it. I had to, too. It was disgusting." The caseworker's voice was shaking, and she was visibly upset by the case.

"Oh my goodness," Kelly said, placing her hand to her mouth, clearly distressed by this news. "Where were the children? Were they in the house with this…"—she trailed off for a second, before completing her question—"…with this mess?"

"Some were. Stephen was in a car, acting as a look out, with one of the mother's boyfriends. When the police came, he ran into the house to warn his mom, and then tried to run away from the police. One of the little girls, who is six years old, was lying on a bed in the basement, with the mother and another boyfriend. The bed was covered in feces, and the mom and other young man were passed out. Two other children were at neighbors' houses, while Timmy was at school. The mother had the children spread out, in case something should happen."

"Where was the father?" I asked.

"We're not sure at the moment. The husband pulled a knife on the mother last week, and has disappeared since. This isn't the children's father; he lives in another state."

"Belinda, the kids didn't seem too upset when they arrived here, which was strange. How were they when they left the house?" I asked.

"Well, we had to locate them. The ones at the house became upset only when the mother began to fight with the police when the children were being taken away. When she woke up to find the police there, she became hysterical."

"Drugs?" Kelly asked.

"Meth," the caseworker answered. "There was a lot of it. There was a Meth lab in the house," she added, in a grim voice. "We weren't able to bring any of the children's clothes or belongings with them, as they were all contaminated with both Meth and feces. I should also mention that both Timmy and Stephen are on lots of prescriptions. Timmy is on five different medications a day, and Stephen is on four a day."

"That seems like a lot," Kelly surmised. Her doctorate in natural medicines left her a little skeptical on the large amounts of prescription medications that many children in foster care were often burdened with.

After signing the paperwork, giving us custody of the children, Belinda thanked us for taking the children in. "I recognize your name," she said to me.

With all seriousness, I said "Police reports, probably. I have been arrested a lot, but not recently."

As my wife sighed, Belinda studied my face hard, before asking timidly, "Are you serious?"

At this, I laughed. "No, not at all."

"Oh. Good," she replied. She continued to study me a few seconds longer, before a look of recognition came across her face. "Are you the Dr. DeGarmo who writes the newsletter and has the website?"

"I am," I responded, surprised by the recognition.

"I thought I knew the name. I get your newsletter; it's really helpful," the caseworker commented. After finishing up the last of the paperwork, we walked her to the door, thanking her for coming. Closing the door behind her, we quickly spread out, checking on the groups of children in the house. Kelly tucked Cassie into bed, and checked on Grace and Brailey, who were also in bed. There was no sleeping, though, as the two were excited about the new additions in the home.

I found Brody downstairs, playing the new air hockey game we got for Christmas from Kelly's mother. Timmy and Alicia were sitting on the couch watching Brody play with Stephen. I allowed them to finish the game before encouraging Brody to attend to his homework. Our three newest were in desperate need of a shower, as all three of them were extremely filthy. As the children began showering, Kelly was on the phone with Hope, answering various questions from her. I went in search of extra pajamas for the three, and began washing the children's clothes and jackets. When they first arrived, I had noticed that the clothing was in rough shape, as is often the case when children from foster care are first placed into our home. What surprised me about this lot of clothing was that much of it was stapled together, and reeked of a smell that I did not want to identify.

Soon, Kolby and Jace returned home from gymnastics. Walking into the house with them was Hope, with several bags of new clothes, shoes, jackets, and school materials, as well as three large pizzas. Giving her a hug, Kelly thanked our friend for her kindness and generosity. The children sat down to eat, with Kolby, Jace, and Brody joining them for a second dinner. It was with interest that I noticed Stephen only eating one piece of pizza, while Timmy and Alicia devoured several pieces, only an hour after they first ate at our house. Though both Kelly and I encouraged the oldest sibling to eat some more, he refused. Was he watching out for his younger brother and sister, ensuring that they got enough? Was he acting like the parental figure? It seemed likely, and was something that Belinda had suggested might be the case.

Nine children posed a small dilemma for Kelly and me that night, as we had to determine who would sleep in what room. I moved a single mattress into Jace's room for Alicia to sleep on, while Kelly readied the guest room for both Timmy and Stephen. As there was only a double mattress in there, the two boys had to sleep together. "Your house is really nice," Timmy said, with a smile on his face. "You really keep it clean." I was surprised by the observation from a young nine-year-old. Stephen once again thanked me for taking us into our home. Before tucking the boys into bed, I led the three of us in prayer, thanking God that they were with us, and asking Him to watch over them in the days and weeks to come. I then crept up the stairs to join Kelly in doing the same with Alicia, who was anxious to give me a hug. By the time Kelly and I got all nine children to bed, it was quite late.

"Do you hear that," my wife said, turning on her side in bed to face me. We had only just made it to bed ourselves and I was looking forward to some sleep. I should have known better, as we had been doing this too long to think otherwise. The sound of crying could be heard from downstairs, which was where I ended up for the next hour, trying to comfort Timmy as he cried himself to sleep. Once more, I felt both powerless to help, and frustrated with birth parents that placed children in such traumatic and frightening experiences.

The next two days went as smoothly as they could, with nine children. Kelly and I were busy each morning, getting each ready for school, preparing breakfast, changing diapers, and driving to every school and day care imaginable in the small town. The evenings were full, as well, yet pleasant. Timmy, Alicia, and Stephen were adjusting well, and Kelly and I quickly grew to love them. We both prepared ourselves for the long haul with the children, as the mother was facing a number of criminal charges. It appeared as if the children were going to be in care for some time.

Yet, as it frequently is in foster care, the unexpected is often the norm, as I found out. "Dr. DeGarmo, the children had court today," Belinda's voice echoed over the phone Friday morning, only three days after the placement.

"Oh, I wasn't aware it was going to be today," I replied. "I like to try to attend if I can," I told her. "I think it sends a positive message to the children that their foster parents care about them."

"Yes, I understand, and we would have told you if we knew about it. It was a bit of a surprise to all of us. Their uncle came down from Maryland last night, and the children were picked up at school this morning for court."

"I see," I said. This was not out of the ordinary. "How did everything go?"

"Well, the judge gave the uncle custody of the children, and they are moving back with him."

"When are they leaving?" I asked. I was not only surprised by the news, I was disappointed.

"Dr. DeGarmo, I am sorry to tell you that they already left."

The news hit me like a hammer. "But we never got to say goodbye. We have boxes of new clothes and shoes for them. Can't they stop by our house before they leave?" I could feel my heart rate begin to speed up.

"I wish they could, but they left an hour ago. This wasn't our decision, and we tried to convince the judge that the children were in a good home, but he said that he wouldn't prevent the children from being with their family. I even went up to the judge at the bench, and said, 'These kids are clean for the first time; they look good, look healthy, and are happy. They are all in homes that love them and can care for them. You ask them yourselves if they want to move. Let them stay here until you find a better place. You haven't even checked this man out.' Unfortunately, the judge only said, 'I'm not keeping them from their family one day longer.'"

My shoulders drooped, as I let forth a heavy sigh. "Okay, well what can you tell me about the uncle?" I asked, hoping to hear that the children were going to a safe and loving environment.

"He has custody of his own two children, from a previous relationship. He is living with his mother, who was abusive in the past," the caseworker said. I could hear her take a deep breath on the other end of the phone line before she hit me with the final piece of information. "He's young; 21 years old."

"Twenty-one years old?" I cried out in dismay. I could feel the anger come over me, and my heart was now racing. "That's too young! How can a 21-year-old take care of not only himself, but seven children, two of them on heavy medications, and one not much younger then himself? I wasn't mature enough to even take care of one child, let alone seven!" I was upset with the judge, and upset with the system, feeling that both had let the children down.

"I understand, Dr. DeGarmo. Unfortunately, the judge felt otherwise," Belinda said, with exhaustion in her voice.

After finishing the conversation with the caseworker, I called Kelly, and delivered the news to her. She was between massages, and took the news hard. I could hear my wife crying on the other end of the phone line, and my heart sank even further. This mother of dozens of children through the years had taken each one into her heart, and each departure from our home had left her heartbroken.

There was little sleeping that night, for either of us. Kelly cried herself to sleep, feeling the sting of this loss particularly strongly. It was hard for her not to say goodbye to the children, and she worried greatly about their new placement and their new home. "Boomie, they might be scared and worried. It's not fair for them, having to go from house to house. What if it were one of our own children? How would someone like Grace feel if she were moved like that, with no explanation? She would be so very scared." With tears rolling down her face, and into her pillow, she sobbed silently to herself. There was little I could do or say to comfort her, as I didn't have the words or wisdom to help her find peace in this.

The knot in my own stomach was strong, as my own grief and frustration left me in a state of depression for the next several days. Not only was I also grieving the loss of these three children, I was angry; angry that these children were placed in this environment. I was angry that I was unable to say goodbye to the children. I was angry, as I felt that the children were not going to get the services or the stability they sorely needed. As an educator, I felt that education was essential for any child's success, and more so for children in foster care. Though Stephen had been in a great deal of trouble at school, he was immensely bright and intelligent. The 13-year-old had been in three fights in the school in the past month, and had a long list of behavior infractions at the school this past year. It was evident that there was very little support from his family in regards to being successful in school. Yet, this kind of support and encouragement was necessary for him to succeed, as it was for both his brother and sister, and all children. I was doubtful that he would receive this type of support and encouragement from his uncle. Besides, I thought, he is also living with his grandmother, who had been abusive to the children's mother. With despair, I believed the children were lost; lost in the sense of them ever having a better future. For years, I had listened as Kelly told me that she wanted to stop fostering, as the sadness she felt each time a child left was too overwhelming for her. It was for the first time that I questioned whether or not I could go on being a foster parent as well.

* * *

"Kelly, Lisa just called, and wants to hold the adoption tomorrow. Call me when you get a chance. Love you. Bye." Leaving a message on her answering machine, I turned to Tim and filled him in.

Tim had joined us for another Up With People reunion, this time joining us not in Europe, but at our home, as we were two days away from having more of our friends join us for that summer's reunion once again in the Georgia mountains. Cassie was just three days from turning one year old, and we were told that the adoption might not go through for another few months. Tim had driven from Arizona to spend some time with us, while several others were coming the next day. Our house was filling up; the anxiety level for the reunion was already high. Lisa's call just moments before added to the anticipation.

"That was the caseworker," I told Tim, who was sitting at the kitchen table, working on some music for the reunion. "She called up to see if we could be ready to adopt both Brailey and Cassie tomorrow."

"Wow, that's great," Tim said, with his usual smile. "I thought Kelly said that you guys weren't going to be able to adopt them for a while."

"Yeah, that's what we were told. Actually, I was still apprehensive that the adoption wasn't going to go through, as we had so many obstacles that almost prevented us from adopting Grace. But, the caseworker just said that everything came together suddenly, and that we could adopt them tomorrow." I was a little stunned myself. I had not permitted myself to feel the joy of adding the two foster children into my family on a permanent basis, due to the fact that, many times, these adoptions do not always turn out successfully for foster parents. Now, with the day of adoption 24 hours away, I allowed the realization that my family was truly going to grow by two more children, and I couldn't stop smiling.

With Brailey dressed in her customary pink frilly dress, and with Cassie in a matching outfit, we stood in front of the judge in his small office in the nearby town that Tuesday morning. Holding Cassie in my arms, I stood close to Kelly, who had Brailey in hers. Surrounding us were Kolby, Jace, Brody, and Grace, along with Tim and the caseworker, Lisa. Unlike Grace's adoption, where a large crowd from our church gathered to join us, the judge's chamber held only us. The elderly judge looked at us with a grin. "Do all of these other children belong to you?"

"Yes, your honor," Kelly replied, beaming. She had warned me several times about making jokes during this adoption, and I obliged. Besides, I was still trying to process the event. After all, my family had just grown by two more children, bringing the number of children with the last name of DeGarmo to six. It mattered not if they were biological or adopted from foster care. To us, it mattered not if they were of "vanilla skin or chocolate skin," as Kelly had coined them. To us, they were simply our children. Regardless of where they came from or how they looked, they were our children.

Chapter 15

I was heading down the rural interstate, driving to the nearby city 30 minutes away. A jumble of emotions was swirling inside of me. Nervousness, excitement, relief, apprehension; I was experiencing them all. After five months, Kelly and I were about to be reunited with Timmy, Alicia, and Stephen. Our family was about to grow once again.

Just a day before, Cathy from DFCS had called the house. I was outside, transplanting some plants to a new location in the garden beds, while Kelly was preparing dinner. After talking with the caseworker, Kelly rang the dinner bell, my cue to come into the house. Heading to the sink to wash the dirt from my hands, I easily noticed the unease in my wife's face. "Everything okay?" I asked.

"Cathy just called," she said, an ever-so-slight smile creasing her face.

"Really? What about?" I replied back. I could feel the blood come to my own face. It had only been a month since we adopted the two girls; a month since we had been foster child free, so to speak. Were we really getting the Call again, so soon?

Before answering, she let out a sigh, in an attempt to release some of the stress she was feeling from the call. "Well, Timmy, Alicia, and Stephen are back in care, along with their two sisters, and Cathy wants to know if we can take them." Again, a nervous smile was only just visible upon her face. "All five of them," she added.

"What? How? All five?" I didn't know what question I wanted answered first.

"Long story short," the Australian began, "the children ended up living with their grandmother, who beat them daily, Cathy said. They were left by themselves from ten in the morning to ten at night, while their grandmother and uncle went to work. Stephen had to basically be their parent, taking care of them. The caseworker in Maryland said that the five children haven't had a chance to be children, and that they just need to go to a home where they can be, and learn how to play. Patsy and Mike just took in that baby, and can't take the other two sisters. Maybe we should…" Kelly's voice trailed off, as she looked to me for my reaction.

I didn't know where to begin. If I wanted to be honest with myself, I had been enjoying the fact that we were not officially foster parents at the moment. I had felt a sense of relaxation and of peace the past month, since the adoption was finalized. Being foster parents was, without a doubt, the hardest thing I had ever done. Yet, at the same time, I also recognized the great need for foster parents; with so many children in care every day, and so very few people willing to bring these children into their homes, the need was great. Perhaps that is why Kelly continued to say yes each time the Call came, despite the many pleas through the years that she was done. Maybe she recognized this need, as well, and was unable to say no to a child in need; a child who was suffering. Maybe this is why she could not say no to a child who simply needed to be loved.

"Five more kids," I finally answered, shaking my head in disbelief. "I don't know, Kel. That would be 11 children in the house. That's crazy!" Despite the smile on my face, I was a little concerned. Could we handle that?

"It is. You're right," she responded, "but what if someone can't take them? What if they need to come here?" There was deep sympathy in her eyes, and I was moved by the depth of compassion my wife felt for children.

"Well, if we have to, but maybe someone else can take care of them. Did Cathy say how long they might be in care for?"

"She said it would probably be a while. There's no other family member who can take them, and their mother still has to go to court for the charges against her from this past spring."

"When are they coming?" There was much needed to be done, I thought to myself.

"Tomorrow night, after school," Kelly replied. "They're flying into Atlanta with a caseworker from Maryland, and will then drive to Covington to meet another caseworker."

So much for our break from fostering, I thought. "Okay, let's do it. Can you call Cathy back, please? I'll go get the guest room ready for the two boys."

"I will," she answered, and began to walk out of the room. An instant later, she turned around, and with tenderness in her voice, asked me, "Boomie, what are we going to do if we take the baby?"

The baby. I was not ready to discuss that possibility, as I was unsure myself. We had found out just a few days earlier that Cassie and Brailey's biological mother was once again pregnant. The news was not unexpected to both Kelly and I, though disturbing. We had already begun to pray for the baby's safety and well-being. Upon hearing the news of a future birth sibling to the two youngest DeGarmos, my wife immediately informed me that she wanted to adopt the infant if it should become possible. Then, when she asked me about the baby, with the possibility of five more children coming, I simply smiled at her, as I was at a loss for words. It seemed that every time the subject of adoption came up, I became a helpless mute.

Now, not even 24 hours later, I was on my way to pick up the three children. Cathy had called earlier that afternoon to inform us that she found a foster home for the two littlest ones, a relief to both Kelly and me. I was not so sure I could handle a full football starting line-up of children in my home. Sure, I had a basketball squad, plus one. These three would bring the team level to a baseball line-up. Eleven, though, seemed almost too much to handle. As I drove along, I found this perspective oddly humorous. Six children seemed quite easy, seven children even manageable, and nine almost too much to handle when compared to 11; funny how one's viewpoint on that belief could change with a little face to-face-experience in the matter.

As I pulled into the child welfare office 25 minutes later, I could feel the emotion of the moment begin to swell inside of me. These three children, who we had considered lost, were now about to be reunited with us. Parking the car, I rapidly jumped out. Giving a very fast hello to the caseworkers, I rushed past them, and embraced Timmy. With tears freely streaming down my face, I then let him go, and enfolded Alicia in a hug, and then Stephen.

"Darn it!" The caseworker was also upset next to me, as I let the warm tears flow unashamed. "I was trying not to cry myself," she said with half a laugh, as the tears began to show in her own eyes. Clearly, the emotion of the moment was a powerful one for all involved.

As I drove home that night with the three children, I thought about how busy Kelly and I were sure to be. Not only was nine children a large number to take care of, but three of these children had been through so much in their young lives, leaving them with a variety of emotional needs and wants. Along with that, we had a baby in diapers, along with five others who also needed a loving mother and father. To be sure, foster parenting was a most difficult adventure; one that often left Kelly and I exhausted physically, emotionally, and mentally. It seemed that our house and our lives were in a constant state of mayhem and chaos. Yet, it was an adventure that also filled our home with much love and laughter. For me, there was no stronger calling in my life than to help these children, a calling that filled my life with joy.